Dogs, Cats &
of Spiritual

Dogs, Cats & Dreams
of Spiritual Awakening

Stephen Wingate

Atma Publishing

Atma Publishing
www.AtmaPublishing.com

Dogs, Cats & Dreams of Spiritual Awakening
Copyright © Stephen Wingate 2007
www.LivingInPeace-TheNaturalState.com
First Printing: January 2007

All rights reserved. No part of this publication may be reproduced or transmitted in any form or by any means, electronic or mechanical, including photocopying, recording or by any information or retrieval system without written permission by the publisher, except for the inclusion of brief quotations in a review.

ISBN-10: 0-9787254-1-7
ISBN-13: 978-0-9787254-1-9

Printed in the USA by Morris Publishing
3212 E. Hwy 30
Kearney, NE 68847
800-650-7888

Cover Design: Clifton A. Hall

Contents

Foreword

It is a privilege to write a few words as a foreword to Stephen's book, *Dogs, Cats and Dreams of Spiritual Awakening*.

I first met Stephen in 2004, not long after I began sharing the 'spiritual pointers' myself. Stephen had been investigating various spiritual teachings over a period of years with the intention of resolving his suffering and doubts. His searching lead him to the teachings of Nisargadatta Maharaj (as presented in the book *I AM THAT*) and from there to the teachings of Nisargadatta's student, 'Sailor' Bob Adamson, currently residing in Melbourne, Australia. Stephen contacted 'Sailor' Bob. Bob suggested that Stephen get in touch with me, since I was in the U.S. sharing the message also.

Within a few weeks, he flew out to see me in Santa Cruz. We met and had a chance to talk over the basics. I reviewed with him the fundamental pointers that I had received from 'Sailor' Bob about our true nature as presence-awareness and how the cause of suffering, questions and doubts arises through believing ourselves to be a separate being apart from that. These were the insights that 'Sailor' Bob shared with me and helped resolve my own searching and suffering.

Now Stephen is moved by a sincere interest to help others who might be struggling with suffering and doubts. Out of his genuine and heartfelt concern to be of help to others, he began to share his understanding with seekers in the Boston area.

As you will find in this book, his talks on the truth of who we are, are consistently direct and to the point. He returns again and again to the important themes of clarifying our identity and resolving the root cause of suffering. While these themes are universal and form the essential message of Nisargadatta Maharaj and 'Sailor' Bob Adamson, Stephen has cast them in his own unique voice. He puts them across with a freshness and clarity that make the message very accessible to a contemporary seeker.

I am delighted to see the publication of Stephen's second book of dialogues. I am sure many will find in these pages clear pointers to the truth of what we are and what we are not.

John Wheeler
Santa Cruz, California
14 December 2006

Introduction

Are you dreaming about Self-Realization, Awakening, Liberation and Enlightenment?

In these dialogues we look into that question together. And what you may find is that what you're seeking, what Self-Realization is, what Awakening is, what Enlightenment is—it's what you already are.

When we're really suffering, it seems to me, and this is what happened with me and with most people—when you're really suffering, you're at the end of your rope and you feel like you can't take it anymore, then you find out. That was my experience. I don't know if that's necessary. But you just can't take it anymore; you can't take living as a separate person.

The ancient traditions point to the fact that at the root of all suffering and seeking is the sense of being separate—separate from our fellow man, separate from God, separate from all of creation. And having to fight, struggle, kick and scratch our way through this life. It's not easy living like that. The spiritual literature says that the end of all spiritual seeking and psychological suffering comes when we see that we're *not* separate, there is no separate person here. And—seeing what you *are* in essence, noticing what you are in essence. It's not an attainment. It's not something new. At the root of psychological suffering and spiritual seeking is a misconception—that is believing you are something you are not.

There's one coin of seeing what you are. There are two sides of that coin. One is seeing what you *are* in your own direct experience, which is very simple. It's not a new state, it's not an attainment. And the other side of the coin is seeing what you are *not*. The misconception of believing and feeling that you are something that you are not is at the root of psychological suffering and spiritual seeking.

When these fundamental pointers are seen clearly, the one coin of what I am, who am I?—then psychological suffering and spiritual seeking fall away. And we awaken to the dream.

Stephen Wingate
Boston, Massachusetts
January 2007

Part I Meeting Dialogues

1

Stay With I Am

Stephen: Most questions come from the perspective of a person who believes himself to be suffering psychologically, and he wants to attain enlightenment because he wants to be an enlightened person. I'm a suffering person now, and I want to do whatever it takes to attain awakening, liberation or enlightenment so I can become an enlightened person.

Suffering is imaginary, and awakening, liberation and enlightenment are also imagination. There is no enlightenment, no awakening, no liberation. There's no person suffering. It's all an imaginary story. All you can confirm in your own direct experience is that you exist, I am. You can confirm that. No one can come to you and say, you don't exist, or you can't say, I don't exist.

'I am' is this presence of awareness, it's not a concept. Everyone here is aware right now. I am aware of these words just like everyone else is. If I hold up a simple object, we can all look at the object, we're all aware of the object. So there's this witnessing presence that we are, and we can call it consciousness, or awareness. We can call it this witnessing presence, or this presence of awareness. It's this sense of being, and you can feel it right now. You have to be here as consciousness to see anything, to hear anything, to feel anything. You have to be here as consciousness. It's not your personal consciousness. Consciousness *is*.

Darren: You know, if I may—when John Wheeler said that, I really got it. I said, oh, I know what you're talking about. And then later on after the group broke up I said, I can get that who I am is not this body and this mind, but when you say that who I am is the same thing for you and me and everybody else, I don't get that.

Stephen: All you know is that consciousness is, I am. That's all you know. This is all I know. I speak from my own experience, and this is what the ancient traditions say, 'I am.' I am the way, the truth and the life, I am. So what is this 'I am' that the ancient traditions are pointing to? It's this sense of being. That can't be denied. As soon as you say, I feel this sense of presence, I get that, but, is yours the same as mine, and the same as others, then you're off into concepts again.

Darren: Well, you know what John said was, if you use your mind, then you can say my consciousness is different from your consciousness. If you don't get your mind involved you might see it is the same consciousness.

Stephen: That's essentially what I just said. So forget about everyone else—for now. That's an interesting intellectual exercise, but stay with this simple presence of being you know exists.

Sharon: May I ask some questions about the concepts you're talking about that are different from my direct experience, and ask whether your experience is different. What you're saying makes sense in that I can say I am a witnessing presence, and my witnessing comes from this spot in the room, and presumably other people's come from other spots in the room. Yet certainly people talk about it all being one. So what is the proof in my direct experience that there's a oneness to this?

Stephen: Stick with what we know, what you know. I know I am. I know there's a witnessing presence—this I am—that I know. Anything that follows I am, I don't know—it's all conceptual, imagination, and speculation.

Sharon: Okay, but it's true that if you stick with 'I am a witnessing presence' there's no psychological suffering.

Stephen: Yes. Now as this witnessing presence, for example, we could have this television on any movie, it doesn't matter what's on. Sometimes we'll focus in on it, and if it's funny, we'll laugh, if it's a horror movie, we'll feel tension, or there may be sadness and we'll cry. So we'll laugh, and we'll cry. There will be pleasure and pain—everything comes and goes. The body and mind are constantly changing. But if we know it's only a movie and we are the witnessing presence of the movie, we're not the character in the movie. So, it's possible to appreciate whatever is happening in the movie as the witnessing presence—whatever happens to this body and mind, whatever imaginary stories come up.

12

As the witnessing presence of it, there's the possibility of appreciating it—we could say loving it. We love the pleasure and the pain, the happiness and the sadness, there's a love of it. But if we think or believe we are the imaginary character playing in the head, we're constantly trying to fix it because we're caught up in the imaginary character, and there's the sense of suffering that happens. Because I want this, and I don't want that, so we're trying to fix the imaginary character all the time.

Everything comes and goes in this witnessing presence. But this witnessing presence is never touched by it.

Darren: I have difficulty when you say the body is imaginary. My body is real. Because to me, even though the body is changing and it will die and dissipate—right here, right now this body is very real.

Stephen: The body comes and goes in your awareness.

Darren: Right, in my awareness, but it is here. There is no denying it.

Stephen: Not all the time.

Darren: Even when I'm not aware of it...

Stephen: As soon as you say that, you're into concepts and imagination.

Darren: Okay.

Stephen: Stick with what we know, I am. This witnessing presence is. This body is only here part of the day—that I'm aware of it. But awareness is here one-hundred percent of the time. So I'm not saying the body is imaginary, I'm saying it's a temporary appearance in what I am. I am always here. The body is not always here, thoughts are not always here, suffering is not always here. But I am—this simple witnessing presence.

And God said unto Moses, I AM THAT I AM: this is my name forever, and this is my memorial unto all generations.—**Exodus**

13

2

The Outrageous Myths of Enlightenment

Darren: So for thousands of years teachers have talked about awakening and enlightenment. What are they talking about? What are they referring to?

Stephen: I like the way Leo Hartong puts it, 'awakening to the dream,' because consciousness doesn't wake up. Consciousness is already awake. You are always this consciousness. It's not that yesterday you were Darren in essence, and one day you become consciousness in essence. You've always been consciousness in essence.

But there was this imaginary story playing that I am Darren, I am the controller of Darren and his story which is imagination. So there's an awakening to the dream—oh, it was all imagination! It's not that you, Darren, as a person will become awakened. It's that this consciousness that you have always been sees the dream as a dream, imagination as imagination. I like Leo Hartong's 'awakening to the dream,' because there's no awakening for the person.

Does consciousness awaken? Consciousness *is*. Does awareness awaken? You were always this simple presence of awareness, this consciousness, this witnessing presence. You were always that. So that doesn't wake up. But you see the imaginary story as an imaginary story.

Darren: So *just that* is what the teachers have been talking about all these years in all the books?

Stephen: Well, you tell me—can consciousness wake up?

Darren: No, no, but I'm just saying that the impression one has, at least I have gotten over the years, is that it is a very blessed moment of ecstasy and bliss, and life is wonderful after that. So, what is the basis of all that?

Stephen: I heard those stories, too, and that's why Stephen, the suffering person, wanted to be Stephen, the enlightened person—because I heard all those stories. But consciousness *is*.

Darren: So they could have made a very simple statement—instead of Buddha sitting under the bodhi tree for years, and people doing all kinds of fancy practices. They could have just said, listen, who you are is just *this*, and that's all there is to it, good bye?

Stephen: That is what they said.

Stanley: Well, that's what Buddha said, 'there is no doer.'

Darren: Buddha said that?

Stanley: Yeah.

Stephen: "Actions happen, deeds are done. There is no individual doer thereof." [That quote has been attributed to Siddhartha Gautama]

Darren: Buddha said that? I didn't realize that.

Stephen: It seems to me, and it's my interpretation, they've all said the same thing. The interpretations are different as the years go on and ideas get built onto the fundamental teachings. But, in essence they all say, consciousness is all there is, the Universal Mind is One, you know, whichever term the different traditions use—I am the way, the truth and the life. I AM THAT I AM.

Darren: I never understood that, I AM THAT I AM.

Stephen: It's just awareness. It's this simple presence of awareness. This is nothing that can be attained, it's nothing that can be lost—it's what you are in essence.

Darren: You know, having gotten that, I think I've gotten that...

Stephen: That's all there is to get. The rest is imagination.

Darren: It seems like that should be conveyable quite easily.

Stephen: Consciousness *is!* I Am! Everybody leave! [laughter] But for some reason all these questions come up: yes, but, what if...

15

Sharon: Well, the people who institutionalized religions noticed there was money in it. They like the money and power, that's why. Most religions are not trying to make you enlightened!

Darren: That's true.

Stanley: It's not to say there aren't people who are awake, but they're in states, or are more inclined to be in certain states of consciousness. But the state is not it. The state is not the thing, but it's often associated with a state.

Suzanne: Oh, like a mystical state, or a state of samadhi—the bliss of samadhi.

Stanley: In fact, I think, and I'm speculating, but I think it's frankly much more likely you're going to experience a certain state if you're not in the mind. But it's just something that would happen like everything else happens. There might be people who are more identified or are more prone to being in a certain state or maybe they're talking to a large group of people and the energy is coming through them so they're in an incredible state—you know.

Darren: And even beyond that they seem to be able to manipulate what's going on—make the blind see and the lame walk. There are all these Indian gurus who do amazing feats.

Stephen: I have a surgeon who did some amazing things to my knees. All of that can happen in the appearance, but there's no individual doing it. It's all an expression of the mysterious source.

Darren: But it seems to be more channeled through those people who are aware of the dream. Like Jesus, he did quite a few amazing things from what I read.

Stephen: That can be a mental or conceptual block, too, because I'm not able to heal the sick or the blind, therefore I'm different from Jesus. But he said, 'I Am,' he didn't say, "I am the healer."

Darren: My question is, do you attach any significance to the fact that once somebody is awake he might be able to move things around a little bit, make the seas calm down.

[laughter]

Stephen: No, everyone is awake. Consciousness is. This awareness is. There's no awake person. Whatever is expressing itself is expressing itself. Apparently some are able to do some interesting mental tricks. Apparently some are able to facilitate the healing of others. But it's not the individual who's doing it.

Darren: I understand that, yes.

Sharon: Right, and it may be that you can do exactly what it is you can do. Maybe you weren't assigned to be Jesus.

Darren: Yes, so I was not programmed to heal others.

Sharon: Yeah, you have other amazing things you can do.

Stephen: If we stick with the simple pointers that in my interpretation all of the ancient traditions are pointing to which is this simple presence of awareness, this 'I am' is what we are—period. Everything else comes and goes. Healings may happen. Mystical experiences may happen. All sorts of events may happen, but *to no one*, and *by no one*—just the awareness, the witnessing presence. So we stick with that, and know ourselves as this witnessing presence.

Realizing my supreme self-nature in the Person of the Witness, the Lord, and the state of desirelessness in bondage or liberation, I feel no inclination for liberation. —**Ashtavakra Gita**

3

Dogs, Cats & the Entertaining Natural State

Sharon: I just now ran an experiment I want to share because it was really fun. First, I thought, well, I can direct my attention—that's the least I can do. So I practiced, you know, I can direct my attention here or there or there. And then I did the opposite. I said, well, why don't I do the opposite and go to a place with no thoughts and see what is the next thought that arises?

So I did that for a little while, and it was kind of fun. Even to isolate what do I mean by the next thought? The next noticeable thought, and just sort of notice, okay, so here's what caught my attention, here's what caught my attention. It was really fun to do. And it started feeling quite good to do that.

Stephen: So you were watching and waiting for what's going to happen next? Yes, that's this witnessing presence that we are. This witnessing presence is watching what's happening.

Sharon: Right, so I'll tell you my list. At one point I thought, okay, it's got to be a really noticeable thought, so I wrote that down. Then I noticed I was having a pleasant sensation in my belly. Then I noticed the sound of your voice—the sound as opposed to the individual words, and I thought, oh, that's interesting. Then I noticed your hand moving. Then you mentioned Leo Hartong, and I thought I better write that down and remember that, and John Wheeler, I'll write him down. And then you said there's no enlightenment, and I thought, oh, I disagree!—it was like an oomph feeling. So then my ear itched. Then someone was speaking vehemently about something and said, "you mean that's all it is?" I'm going to write that down.

It was kind of fun to see what my mind would notice. There were lots of things I noticed but couldn't write down because there was the whole of it. There was the whole of things going on. So I'd just write down the things that sort of grabbed my attention.

Darren: I can see if one does what Sharon just did, life could be quite entertaining. It's like, okay, let's see what's going to show up next.

Stephen: That *is* your natural state—the way she described it. That is the natural state.

Darren: It's almost how animals live.

Stephen: Yes, I think that's safe to say. I think cats and dogs are the best examples of this. You can see a lot by observing a cat. Why doesn't a cat have psychological suffering?

Darren: Many years ago when I did the EST training, they said when a dog gets hit by a car it yelps and screams, barks and licks its wound, and then limps away. He doesn't make up a story about how the driver was this and that, or this shouldn't be happening. It just happened, right now this happened and I'm going to see what I can do to reduce the pain, and he goes on with his life.

Stephen: Yes, psychological suffering is all imaginary. There's no person who can suffer psychologically without imagination. There's no person who can be enlightened without imagination. All there is, is this witnessing presence, this I am. That's all that's real, and that's what you are. Everything else is imagination, speculation, conceptualization... [laughing]... those are some big words!

So, it's this simple. Consciousness is your essence—the Natural State. You can't attain it, you can't lose it. You can't get rid of it. You can't meditate yourself into it. It just *is*. And there's no suffering.

You shall no longer take things at second or third hand, nor look through the eyes of the dead, nor feed on the specters in books. You shall not look through my eyes either, nor take things from me. You shall listen to all sides and filter them from your self. —**Walt Whitman**

4

Everything is Happening to No One

Raymond: So you are totally or strongly identified with awareness?

Stephen: No. Awareness *is*. Consciousness *is*. There's no 'I' who's identified with consciousness. The only thing that can be verified is that consciousness *is*. There's no Stephen who is identified with consciousness. I am consciousness. There's this is-ness. Is-ness is.

Raymond: Okay. Let me put it a different way.

Stephen: Okay.

Raymond: What's happening or arising now, compared to before when you were still seeking?

Stephen: All the stories have lost their edge and their bite. Imagination is free to come and go. The stories are free to come and go through consciousness. Whereas before there was an attempt to fix the stories, and to fix the imaginary character, Stephen. Previously I wanted my story to be better than it was, and I felt I had to fix it. But there is no separate controlling entity or ego here who can control the stories or control anything else. So, consciousness is.

Raymond: And that absence of trying to control or fix the story happens effortlessly?

Stephen: Yes.

Raymond: It happens without you saying anything, or just once in a while you might notice that, you know...

Stephen: It's like watching a television show. If you're watching a show or you're in a situation that's uncomfortable, you change the channel. I don't like this situation so I'm leaving. If I'm watching something on television that's disturbing, I change the channel.
   The story doesn't matter. The story comes up, and who cares about the story? Sometimes it's a happy story, or a sad story. You know it's

20

going to pass. The story can be happy for a while—oh, I like this, things are going the way I like them—it's going to pass. And then some other story will come along that you don't like, but that will pass. And then there will be a story to which you're indifferent—whatever. And that will pass.

All the stories come and go. But what doesn't come and go is this witnessing presence that I am, and we all are. And that's the peace, this I am, this witnessing presence is the peace that's at peace with the war stories. This peace is at peace with war. This peace is at peace with peace. Everything is as it is.

And everything is happening, but to no one. That's a good one. Everything is happening, but to no one. Everything is happening, to no one—so what a relief.

You need not bring your dream to a definite conclusion, or make it noble, or happy, or beautiful; all you need is to realize you are dreaming. On waking up you find you are love itself, embracing all.
—**Nisargadatta Maharaj**

Awakening to the Dream

Stephen: The thought 'I am not enlightened' is no more or less valid than the thought 'I am enlightened.' They're both equally invalid, they're irrelevant. 'I have to get this understanding' or 'I already have this understanding'—both irrelevant. They're just thoughts, meaningless and empty. They don't touch this witnessing presence that you are. 'I am enlightened,' 'I am not enlightened'—what? Consciousness *is*.

Darren: But 'I am enlightened' is a simple way of saying that consciousness at this location is aware of the dream as being a dream. So if I say, "I am enlightened," what I'm trying to say is that for all these years this body-mind combination wasn't aware that this dream is just a dream, and now the consciousness here realizes that the dream has always been a dream.

Stephen: But I don't want to portray a story of an *un*enlightened person, and thinking tomorrow I'm going to be an enlightened person.

Darren: Well, in this context you could say that.

Stephen: Well, I know what you mean, but it sets up false expectations and people want to be an enlightened person. See there's no person there. See that all there is, is I am, this witnessing presence, and then you won't have any interest in enlightenment. Who cares about enlightenment? It's just an idea. See that consciousness *is*, and you won't have any interest in enlightenment. As soon as it's said, oh, yes, I'm enlightened and I'm going to teach you how to be enlightened, that's nonsense. It sets up false expectations. It implies you're missing something.

Darren: Well, there is something missing, right? What you're missing is the truth. Because five years ago, ten or twenty years ago you didn't realize you were living a dream, and now you realize you were living a dream—so, just that. It's very subtle.

Stephen: I see, but it's presented in other ways I don't agree with. Like, "I'm enlightened and I'll teach you how to be enlightened"—that's nonsense. Consciousness *is*. Can consciousness attain consciousness? Can awareness attain awareness? You are this consciousness. But there can be an awakening to the dream.

Why this talk of attaining and not attaining? The matter is thus—by thinking of something you create an entity, and by thinking of *nothing* you create another. Let such erroneous thinking perish utterly, and then nothing remains for you to go seeking! **—Zen Master Huang Po**

The Fall from Grace

Darren: I was telling Walter that your message is mainly about putting an end to suffering—that's what you got, right? You put an end to your own suffering.

Stephen: There are two points that have come out of this. Because the question arises, why do I have these meetings? There are two reasons: one is to share the fact that it's possible to be free of psychological suffering, and the second is that it's possible to be free of spiritual seeking. And I say that because it's my experience. I was experiencing psychological suffering, and I was seeking spiritually to overcome the suffering. That was the story of my life.

Darren: Do you make a distinction between psychological suffering and emotional suffering?

Stephen: Well, they get resolved together. I can talk about the insight or recognition that happens and it's nothing new. It seems to me that all the ancient traditions are pointing to this—seeing what you are in essence, noticing what you are in essence. It's not an attainment. It's not something new. At the root of psychological suffering is a misconception—that is believing you are something you are not.

There's one coin of seeing what you are. But there are two sides of that coin. One is seeing what you *are* in your own direct experience, which is very simple. It's not a new state, it's not an attainment. And the other side of the coin is seeing what you are *not*. The misconception of believing and feeling that you are something you are not is at the root of psychological suffering. When this is seen clearly, the one coin of what I am, who am I?—then psychological suffering and spiritual seeking fall away.

Walter: Would you say that psychological suffering is a result of identifying with your body/mind?

Stephen: Yes. If you look in your own direct experience, and I speak from my own experience and we're all essentially the same. The human experience is essentially the same for all of us. At the root of psychological suffering is believing, thinking, feeling, and sensing that you are the person, the body/mind organism.

Walter: Yes, the ego.

Stephen: The ego, the sense of being separate.

Walter: Exactly.

Stephen: We can look in our own experience and see anytime and every time we're experiencing psychological suffering, at the root of the suffering is 'me'! When there's no 'me' there's no psychological suffering. That's one of the first points we notice about psychological suffering. At the root of it is this ego, this I, this sense of being a separate person—Walter, Darren or Stephen. We give it a label and a name.

Walter: Ramesh uses the phrase 'dis-identifying with the ego-self.'

Stephen: When it's seen clearly, this ego-self—and we can broaden the definition of it—it's an image of a body/mind, it's a story, it's a belief in the existence of a separate, controlling entity. That's the sense of being separate, this sense of ego. Not only am I a separate body/mind organism, but I'm a separate, *controlling* entity. Somehow I was able to separate myself from the rest of creation, and now I'm able to exercise control over the universe.

If we look in our own direct experience, we'll see that the belief in the ego, the existence of a separate, controlling entity is at the root of all psychological suffering. What's happening when psychological suffering is happening? We notice there's a story playing in the head, and the story revolves around *me*. I'm not good enough. I need to improve my life. I need to be a better person. I need to be more spiritual. I need to be more loving and kind. I need to be a better parent, a better brother, a better father—it all revolves around *me*.

Darren: So if that is the mistake, what is the correct way of viewing it?

Stephen: Every time psychological suffering is happening, there's a story playing. There's a series of images and a story playing. And the story revolves around me—Stephen, Walter, Darren. We see this in our

25

own experience. So the suggestion is to look into and find out who am I? Ramana suggested this and many others.

Walter: One way of putting it is I am not Walter; I am that which is aware of Walter and what's happening.

Stephen: Seeing that in your own direct experience, yes—but, not just conceptually. So we sit here and we say, okay, my interest is in being free of psychological suffering and spiritual seeking. I've read Nisargadatta, Ramana, the New Testament, the Old Testament, and most of the ancient scriptures. They all say that at the root of suffering is the belief you are separate from God, separate from Consciousness, separate from Intelligence-Energy, whatever word you're comfortable with.

If we look in our own direct experience, and ask, who am I? What is this me that I think I am? We notice at the root of psychological suffering is this 'me' character. The assumption is this me exists as a separate entity who can exercise its own control. So we sit here and we look, and ask, is that true? Is there any separate, controlling entity? Is there any separate ego, any separate Walter that exists as a separate controlling entity?

Darren: We are separate body/minds, right?

Stephen: Nothing is separate. Absolutely nothing is separate. If you remove one atom of hydrogen from the water molecules in your body it will fall apart.

Darren: But there's a physical body over there, a body over here, and over there. There is a distinct separation.

Stephen: There is no separation until the I-thought arises. When there's no thinking, there's no separation. There is no separation, it's only conceptual.

Looking in your own direct experience you see there's no suffering unless there's a belief in this ego, this me. So, the suggestion is to look and see if that's true. Is there any separate ego, any separate Walter, any separate Darren, any separate me who can exercise control?

We notice this me, this Stephen I thought I was, is nothing more than an image, it's a concept, a story. It's a belief in the existence of Stephen as a separate entity. So we're sitting here and we ask

26

ourselves, what is this me that I think I am? Can I find anything I can point to and say, this is me? Is there any separate, controlling entity here at all? And it's seen in your own experience that this me, this ego I thought I was is nothing but an image. It's a series of stories, thoughts, memories, beliefs—it's all conceptual. It's seen that's all it is. It has no separate existence.

Walter: But Darren's point is that there are three individuals sitting here—you, me, and Darren.

Stephen: There are three points of consciousness. Nothing is separate. Nothing is separate in the universe.

Walter: No, but there are three individuals sitting here.

Stephen: There are three points of consciousness.

Walter: Ramesh uses the phrase, 'we are dreamed characters in a dreamed world.'

Stephen: You are the dreamer, the dream characters, and the dreaming. There's no separation.

Walter: Right.

Stephen: We can notice in our own direct experience that Darren, Stephen or Walter, the character we think we are, is imaginary. We want to look into this because we notice that every time we're suffering, there's this character in a story that's playing in the head. It's imagination. When there's no imagination, when there's no imaginary Walter, when there's no story playing, there's no suffering!

Darren: Let me ask you this, if I find my wife cheating on me, how would I not suffer by recognizing that I don't exist as an ego?

Stephen: We can talk about specific hypothetical situations, but let's stay with the basics of what I am and what I am not. That will answer all of the specific situations that arise.

Darren: Okay, I see what you're saying.

Stephen: We could come up with an infinite number of specific hypothetical situations to address.

Darren: I'm good at that.

Stephen: And they are all resolved by this insight.

Darren: If I see I am not a controlling entity, then what I say or do, or what happens through me is not a result of my own will.

Stephen: There is no one there doing anything. Everything is happening.

Darren: How does one see that?

Stephen: By looking to your own experience. We'll continue looking at the coin of what I am. One side is what I am, and the other side is what I am not. We want to resolve that question from the positive perspective of what I am, and from the negative perspective of what I am not. We want to look at both sides.

We've seen that at the root of psychological suffering is the belief in the existence of a separate entity. We want to look into that belief in our own experience. Is there any separate entity here? Is there any separate, controlling entity? Is there any separate will here? Was this body/mind organism somehow able to separate itself from the rest of creation, and then exercise control over the rest of the universe? Is there any way this body/mind organism could separate itself from whatever created the universe, and then exercise its own separate will—is that possible?

Darren: Well, you know, if one looks in one's own experience, it seems that we do have free will.

Stephen: And that is at the root of psychological suffering—that belief and that sense.

Darren: I chose to come here this evening, and I came here. It seems it was my will, my decision, right?

Stephen: If we look into this 'me' that says 'my' will, what do we find?

Walter: Now, stop right there. Did he choose to come here?

Stephen: Let's look into that. We could answer conceptually, but it doesn't help. It's not a belief.

Walter: Never mind all that. Just answer—did he choose to come here?

Stephen: There is no separate Darren who chose to come here.

Walter: Did Darren choose to come here tonight?

Stephen: No.

Walter: Alright. That's alright. I'll buy that.

Darren: You buy that, Walter?

Walter: Yes. I asked Francis Lucille that question the first time I met him. I said, Francis, I'm here tonight. Did I choose to come here? He said, no. You couldn't have been anywhere else. Everything in the universe conspired for you to be here.

Stephen: Exactly.

Darren: That means the universe conspired to have everything happening everywhere.

Stephen: Whatever is moving the universe caused you to be here tonight. The Mysterious Source of all existence, God, Universal Intelligence, Consciousness, Awareness—whatever word we want to call it. It's a mystery. We can all agree it's an absolute mystery that's moving the universe.

The Mysterious Source of all existence moves everything. There's no possible way any entity could separate itself. There is no entity in the universe that could separate itself from the Mysterious Source of all existence and then exercise control—it's just not possible. You can look in your own direct experience and see it's true. In your own daily experience—thoughts happen, feelings happen, sensations happen, and actions happen. The sun shines, the earth turns, the universe moves—there's no separate entity doing any of that. In your own direct experience, whatever thought, feeling or sensation is happening, it's the Mysterious Source creating that thought, feeling, and sensation—there's no separate entity doing any of it.

Darren: Walter, do you feel that way in your own life? That everything you have done was not a result of your own free will?

Walter: Yes, Ramesh makes that point. He says if you really look back in your life you'll find you didn't control the decisions. I think it's true. It's an intellectual exercise, but I think it's true.

Stephen: There is no separate entity who could possibly exercise its own will. It's not possible for Darren to separate himself from the rest of creation. It's not possible for the body/mind to be born into the world, to separate itself from the rest of creation, and then exercise its own separate will. Whatever is expressing itself through this body/mind organism called Darren is the same Mysterious Essence that's expressing itself through the cat, through Walter, through Stephen, through every tree, flower, and blade of grass. The Mysterious Source is expressing itself. Darren is not expressing himself. There is no separate Darren.

Darren: Would you say the moment one sees that to be the truth that would be enlightenment?

Stephen: Seeing that you are not this separate ego, this me is one side of the coin. Then we say, well, what am I? My entire life I thought I was this Stephen character.

Walter: But answer his question. I think the answer is yes.

Stephen: I am answering his question. There are two sides to this coin. It's one coin, what I am. But it's important to see both sides of the coin—what I *am* and what I am *not*. So, we see what I am not—I am not a separate entity. But my whole life I felt I was a separate ego. So what am I? Now we look and see what is it about me that can't be denied? What is it about me that's always true? What is it about me that's never changed? What we notice is that from the time we were a little child and up to now, there's this awareness—right now! You can always notice it.

Seeing is happening. Hearing is happening. The senses are active. There's an awareness of the seeing, the hearing, and the senses. There's an awareness of all that. We can look back and consider our whole life. There's always been this awareness, this consciousness that I am. Everything comes and goes, we could say, through this awareness—there's *no through*, or in or out, but just to put it into words. Our entire life everything has gone through this awareness. Our life story is always changing. The body is always changing. The mind, thoughts are always changing; feelings are always changing; sensations are always changing. Our body and mind, and our experiences are always changing.

What is it about me that has never changed? What's always the same? We notice it's this consciousness that I am. I am this consciousness. It's this witnessing presence. It's watching. It's watching the body as it grows older. Sometimes the body is healthy and sometimes it's sick. It watches the thoughts. Sometimes there are pleasant thoughts, and sometimes there are unpleasant thoughts. It watches the feelings—they're the same, always changing.

Walter: Back to Darren's question, Ramesh would constantly say, everything that's happening is the impersonal functioning of totality.

Stephen: Yes, there are a lot of different ways to say 'impersonal functioning of totality.' It's the same as God, or Universal Intelligence. There are a lot of different words and phrases we can use to point to the same Mystery.

Darren: Walter, if you can see it's just the impersonal functioning of totality, and you had no say in the matter of what you did, nor did anybody else, you cannot feel guilt.

Walter: That's true.

Darren: And you cannot hate somebody else.

Walter: No.

Darren: Because it was not them.

Walter: You cannot condemn. You cannot criticize. I agree—if you hold that view.

31

Darren: Can you do that Walter?

Walter: Oh, no. That's why I hang around people like this.

Darren: Can you do that, Stephen?

Stephen: I'm doing nothing. Everything is happening. Whatever is happening is happening. This is the peace that's at peace with war. This is the love that loves hate. This is unconditional and absolute. This witnesses the peaceful experiences and the experiences of war. It's not relative. It's not good or bad. It's not good or evil. It's not peaceful or war-like. It's the witnessing presence. It's absolute. It's unconditional—this consciousness, this awareness that I am.

Whatever is happening is happening. There is no one who's ever done anything. It's not as though this insight happens and you'll start to do nice things. It's not a personal doing. Whatever is happening is happening.

Darren: So, Hitler doesn't deserve anymore condemnation than Mother Theresa deserves praise.

Stephen: Not personally, however, if Hitler or Charles Manson comes into the room, it's not safe for us to be here with them. We'll want to separate them from society. But they're not personally doing anything. The Mysterious Source is expressing itself as Hitler and Mother Theresa. There's no personal blame. If this cat starts biting us, we'll move the cat into the other room, but we don't blame the cat personally.

Darren: Right.

Stephen: So everything is happening.

Darren: Does that point of view take away our loving another. For example, if the cat does nice things we cannot even love it because it's not the cat doing anything. Something else is doing it through the cat.

Stephen: It's impersonal. Love is impersonal. It's not I love you, but there is love. In personal relationships there can be special relationships, but there's not a special love. There can be a special attraction based on biological and psychological compatibility. It's not a personal doing, it just happens.

Darren: This is the first time I've ever heard someone say that compatibility is personal, but love is impersonal.

Stephen: You can see in your own experience that you are more compatible with some people than with others. That happens. It's not something you can do. Either an attraction happens or it doesn't. You don't create the spark or the attraction to another person. Either it happens or it doesn't. Even personal relationships are not a personal doing. The ego is not a creation of the ego. It's an expression of the Mysterious Source. Even the ego is a creation of the Mysterious Source. The Mysterious Source created the appearance of the ego and its falling away. The Mysterious Source is moving everything, and is not separate from anything.

Darren: The ego falls away?

Stephen: It's seen clearly as not being who I am.

Darren: Okay, when you see it clearly.

Stephen: It's seen as an appearance. This Stephen character is an appearance in awareness, just like these hands are an appearance. I see these hands moving in front of me. I also see Stephen the character. It's not who I am. I am the witnessing presence. I am the consciousness, the awareness. So that's the other side of the coin. It's seeing who I am. If I am not this separate ego character then what am I? Who am I?

Darren: I see that if one can adopt that view, then one cannot condemn anybody.

Stephen: Not personally, no.

Darren: Yes.

Stephen: But Charles Manson is a dangerous man, and we want to separate him from society. But we don't blame him personally and say, how can you behave like that? How can you kill others? We know his behavior is just happening. It would be like asking a Pit Bull...

Darren: Why do you bite?

Stephen: Yes, why are you biting people? It's happening. It's like asking a cat, why do you meow?

Darren: Okay, so if one was to get that, are you saying that would be the end of suffering?

Stephen: Notice in your own experience, what's happening when psychological suffering is happening? There's a story playing that revolves around 'me', this Darren character. What if it's seen that this Darren character is just an image, it's just a story? So it's seen that any time there's psychological suffering happening, there's a story playing in the head, an upsetting story that creates an uncomfortable energy in the body—and we call that experience psychological suffering. So we see it's just a story playing about this Darren character, and it's just an image.

There is no separate, controlling entity called Darren. There is just consciousness watching the show. What I am is this consciousness. So now I know myself as I am—as consciousness—this I am-ness which is right now. It's not *I was*, or *I will be*—it's *I am!* This consciousness *is*, and this is what I am. And you notice in your own experience that at any given point in time this consciousness is here. It's always here, and it's always now. So you know this is what I am.

Everything else about Darren changes. His body and mind are always changing. His thoughts are changing. His feelings are changing. His sensations are changing. Everything is changing. But what always remains the same is this consciousness that I am. Now I know myself as I Am. I am the way, the truth and the life. I am That. I AM THAT I AM. This is what the ancient traditions are pointing to—this I Am— this consciousness that *is*. And we are already That. So this is not an attainment. It's a recognition, a realization of what *I am*. And it's a recognition of what *I am not*. The belief in what I am not, this separate character called Darren, or Walter, or Stephen—this image is at the root of all psychological suffering. The separate character is nothing more than a concept, an image, a story. So all psychological suffering is based in imagination.

34

Darren: Let me ask you this—let's put this to the test and see where the rubber hits the road. If I'm clear that who I am is this witness to all that's happening to the body/mind, and this body/mind's wife cheats on him, the stock market crashes and I get wiped out, my children are kidnapped—all bad things happen. Even if I step out and see I'm only a witness to all of this happening, there is still suffering. Wouldn't there be suffering—losing your children, your wife, your money?

Stephen: Notice this in your own experience—the body/mind organism lives in the world of opposites. It lives in the world of pleasure and pain, happiness and sadness, laughter and tears. That continues on, but there's no one doing that. There's a new perspective on the pleasure and the pain. There's a new perspective on the laughing and the crying. There's a new perspective on everything that happens to the body/mind organism—there's a new perspective.

Everything that happens—the pleasure and pain, the happiness and sadness, the laughter and tears, the success and failure, continue happening as they've always been happening. But there's a new perspective on it all. It's all witnessed. So pleasure and pain continue to happen. Happiness and sadness—all of that continues to happen, but it's witnessed. I am not that, I am the witness of that.

Walter: Let me ask a clarifying question. Darren is sitting here and we just learned the stock market crashed and he's wiped out. He heard you say that what he really is, is not the body/mind, he's the awareness of it. The question is, is he going to suffer?

Darren: I am going to suffer.

Walter: Right. I quite agree. You are going to suffer.

Stephen: Who is going to suffer?

Walter: He is, Darren, the guy in the blue shirt. He's just been wiped out!

Stephen: What are you in essence? Are you Darren?

Darren: The ego you mean?

Stephen: Yes, or are you the witness of Darren and his story? This gets to the root of it. This is seeing what I am in essence.

Darren: I see that I am both. I see I can be the witness, and at the same time I am this body/mind organism.

Stephen: Yes, you are both. But what are you in *essence*? What is your essence? What is it about you that doesn't change? The body/mind organism is always changing.

Darren: The awareness doesn't change.

Stephen: The stock market goes up, you're happy. The stock market goes down, you're sad. What is it about you that was never happy, or sad? What is it about you that witnesses the happiness and the sadness?

Darren: Who I am.

Stephen: The awareness is what I am.

Darren: Right, okay.

Stephen: So that's the new perspective. If there's a belief that I am this Darren character in essence there will be suffering. You are Darren, but it's not your essence.

Darren: I see what you're saying. I wouldn't be as attached. If I think that all I am is this body/mind, when the market crashes it's much more severe than if I see who I am in essence is not this body/mind. The loss to this body/mind is not as significant as it would be if all I was is this body/mind.

Walter: May I suggest that until you're enlightened, hearing him say you're not the body/mind is not going to affect your suffering if the stock market wipes you out. Until you are enlightened! To hear him say that won't help.

Stephen: Seeing this in your own direct experience is the practical matter. We can talk about enlightenment as a concept. There is a concept of enlightenment. I'd like to share the illustration of the pendulum.

36

Darren: The Wayne Liquorman example?

Stephen: Yes. A pendulum swings from the fulcrum at the center. If you believe you are the ego, it's like living at the bottom of the pendulum. You experience the full effects of swinging from happiness to sadness, happiness to sadness. When you know yourself as consciousness, it's like living up here at the fulcrum. You watch the swings of happiness and sadness. You are up here at the fulcrum. When the stock market crashes, Darren is sad. The body/mind organism is sad, of course it's sad—you just got wiped out! But you know I am the witnessing presence, and I'm watching the sadness just like you're watching a movie on television—that's the difference.

If you're watching a movie on television and you believe you are the character in the movie, you're absolutely convinced, there's not even a question of doubt, you are the character in the movie and you're being attacked, then of course you're going to suffer along with the character. As soon as it's pointed out you are not the character in the movie, you're watching the character in the movie, there's a sense of relief. Now you're watching the movie as the witnessing presence of the movie. There is happiness, sadness, and all the human emotions.

Darren: But not as intense.

Stephen: They're witnessed. You're living at the fulcrum up here. We can look into this concept of enlightenment and ask, what is it? What I am in essence is this consciousness. I'm not separate from God. There is no separation. I am not separate from awareness, consciousness, life itself.

Darren: I don't get that. Even if I get that who I am in essence is this witnessing awareness, I don't know, or there's no way to know that this witnessing presence is the same witnessing presence looking through your eyes.

Stephen: If someone says, prove to me we are not separate, I say prove that we are separate! Let's consider this illustration. There's one body here [referring to the speaker's body], there's one body of awareness with different points of consciousness. If I strike my left hand with a hammer, the left hand will hurt, but not the right hand. There is one body of awareness here with different points of consciousness. If I strike my knee with a hammer, the knee hurts.

37

There's a point of consciousness at the knee. There is one body of awareness with different points of consciousness. So, in this room there are three people who are different points of consciousness of the One Universal body of Awareness.

Darren: Yes, but I think perhaps one needs to have this enlightenment experience to get that it's the same awareness.

Stephen: When does the appearance of separation happen? There is no separation, there's not even the idea of separation until the first thought arises. When there's no thought, there's no separation. In your own experience when you wake up in the morning, prior to the first thought, the thought, 'I' have to get up for work, 'I' have to get up for breakfast, 'I'... prior to that first thought...

Darren: There is no separation.

Stephen: There's just absolute awareness! There's no separate entity at all. As soon as the I-thought arises and the image of Stephen, Darren, or Walter, that is the birth of the appearance of separation. In your own experience just before you wake up in the morning, you can notice this yourself. You'll notice the first thought is 'I' and then whatever follows. 'I' sense the sunlight through the window. 'I' hear the alarm clock. Or 'I'...

Darren: So what you're saying is prior to...

Stephen: Prior to thought.

Darren: It's all one.

Stephen: There's no separation prior to thought. So the next question is, does thought actually divide the universe, and separate me from you, or does it just appear so? So we see there is no separation. Separation is only a thought. The birth of the appearance of separation is this first thought, this I-thought and I-image.

We notice that in our own experience when we wake up in the morning. When you wake up in the morning you'll notice the thoughts 'I' hear the alarm clock. What witnessed that first thought? What was there that witnessed it? It's absolute awareness. Absolute awareness wakes up into relative consciousness with the first thought, 'I', 'I am.'

38

'I am' is a pointer to this relative consciousness that I am. There are no problems as I am. It's when I am Walter and his story, I am Darren and his story, I am Stephen and his story—that is the birth of the potential for psychological suffering—this 'I am' thought followed by a story about me.

So we look and ask, is this thought 'I am' truly separating all of creation into separate little I ams, separate little entities, or does it just appear so? And we notice in our own experience when we wake up in the morning this I-thought arises. What is there that witnesses this I thought? That's what I am in essence. I am this witnessing presence, this awareness—this is what I am.

Darren: Okay, so let me ask you this—once you get really clear that who you are is not this body/mind called Stephen, but you are the witnessing presence, and who you really are is not separate from anyone or anything else, if someone comes along and says, I'm going to take your computer and I'm going to take your girlfriend, then you could say, well, fine. What would stop you from doing that?

Walter: Doing what?

Darren: What would stop you from saying, you can have my computer, my girlfriend, my home, everything. If who you are is everybody else, there's no distinction. If who you are is the witnessing awareness.

Walter: Interesting question.

Darren: What would stop you from saying, no, you cannot take my money or my property?

Stephen: Maybe that happens or maybe it doesn't happen.

Darren: You mean in some cases one would say, okay, you can have it all?

Stephen: We can consider the behavior of different characters throughout history who have expressed this. Some appear to be completely detached from the body/mind organism and they'd sit and do absolutely nothing. People had to come and feed them.

39

Darren: Like Ramana.

Walter: Want me to give you Ramesh's answer to that? First of all, I'll tell you the answer he gave to the man who asked, if I have no control over my actions, what's to stop me from going out and killing someone on the street? Ramesh's answer was, you couldn't possibly do that. But Ramesh says, to answer your question, you don't control your thoughts, you don't generate your thoughts. Your thoughts come to you from consciousness, and you react to those thoughts according to your genes and your conditioning. That's why he says you have no control over your actions.

Darren: Even after you see that who you are is this witnessing presence?

Walter: Yes.

Darren: Your body/mind organism is still responding to thoughts.

Walter: Thoughts that come from consciousness, and you respond according to your genes and your conditioning.

Darren: That's what Stephen is saying. In some instances one would say, fine, you can take my property. In other instances, one might say, no. Okay, I see what you're saying.

Stephen: When you ask, how will you respond to specific hypothetical situations like if the stock market crashes, or if your wife leaves you—there's a new perspective on those events. The perspective is that I am not reacting to the stock market crash. I'm not reacting to losing my wife. I'm the witnessing presence that's watching this conditioned body/mind respond to those events.

The behavior may change in this body/mind organism. It may change—you may be more loving and kind, or maybe you won't. There's no way to know how the Mysterious Source of all existence will express itself. It has always been expressing itself. It's not as though Darren has been expressing himself for the past forty years, and now Consciousness, God or Intelligence Energy will on this day begin expressing itself. It's realized that all there is, is this consciousness expressing itself. So whatever happens, happens.

There may be changes in your behavior or maybe not. But there's a new perspective—as illustrated with the pendulum example. If I am Stephen, then I'm the one who's responsible for whether I'm happy or sad, or if I'm successful or I fail. So I'm living at the bottom of the pendulum. Sometimes I get things right, and sometimes I don't get it right. So I'm always in flux.

Darren: So the closer you get to being more and more convinced that who you are...

Stephen: Just see it now! There's no degree of convincing. There's the recognition that you can't possibly be a separate entity—it's not possible. Everything is happening! You can debate whether there's free will or destiny. But what can't be debated is that this consciousness *is*—I am. So you know yourself as this consciousness, this witnessing presence that's watching the show. Then whatever happens in the show is witnessed. But there's no sense that I'm doing anything. The source of the words that are coming out of this mouth right now is an *absolute mystery*. There's no way to know where anything comes from. So we call it the Mysterious Source because it's a mystery. What makes the cat meow?

Darren: Walter, you buy that, right?

Walter: To get back to Darren's question, if the stock market crashes, is he going to do anything?

Stephen: What do you mean?

Walter: Will he do anything about it.

Stephen: As you said, whatever this body/mind organism is conditioned to do it will do. But there's a new perspective on it. If there's a belief that I am Darren, I am in control, I'm a separate entity, then there's a different experience—there are big swings in your experience. But knowing yourself as this consciousness, there's the recognition that I'm not doing anything.

If the stock market crashes, and Darren responds with sadness and despair, that's witnessed. Oh, look at the sadness and despair! Or if the response is a detached feeling, that's witnessed. Oh, look at the detached feeling. The stock market crashed and yet the body/mind

41

organism is detached. Isn't that amazing! There's a witnessing of this body/mind organism. There's no sense that I'm in control. There's no Stephen here making these finger nails grow. There's no Stephen here making these words come out. Where are these words coming from? If you punch me, I have no idea what will happen—I may punch back or I may run—I don't know. But it's not me doing it, there's no separate entity doing anything.

Darren: When you became clear about that, how did that affect your life?

Stephen: There was a belief in this Stephen character who existed as a separate, controlling entity. So there were big swings in trying to take control of my life—going to retreats and seminars, going to see teachers, trying to become enlightened because I wanted to be free of psychological suffering.

So it was seen that this Stephen character is just a story that's playing! There is no separate entity called Stephen, it's just an image. What I am is this consciousness. So the spiritual seeking comes to an end. There's no one here doing anything, there's just a story.

The suffering is in trying to become enlightened. That is the very suffering from which I wanted to be free. I'm not good enough. Stephen, this ego, is not good enough so I have to become enlightened. The suffering is in struggling with *what is*, struggling with life. At the root of the suffering is the sense that I'm separate, in control, and I can exercise control if I go to enough teachers, if I meditate enough, if I read enough books—I personally will become enlightened. That's seen to be false.

There is no one to become enlightened. There's just consciousness. I am this consciousness watching Stephen trying to become enlightened. It's seen to be a joke! It's a joke! There's no one to become enlightened, and there was no one ever suffering. It was all a story.

All that exists is consciousness, this witnessing presence watching the whole show. I am the witnessing presence. So the psychological suffering falls away. The spiritual seeking falls away. There's no one to do anything. There's this witnessing presence watching it all. So for me there was a sense of relief.

Darren: Was it like a euphoric reaction?

Stephen: No.

Darren: Almost like a non-event. For example, if you had lost all your money in the stock market before, and if you lose everything today—what is different about your experience now?

Stephen: There's no way to know. But the difference now is that I just watch what happens. I am the witnessing presence of whatever happens. I may be upset, or I may be detached, and there's a witnessing of whatever happens. Oh, look, there's a feeling of detachment. I lost everything I own, and there is absolutely no response, wow! Or I may be dejected and sad. And I'll notice the sadness.

There's no sense that I *shouldn't* be sad, or I *should be* detached. I need to meditate more. If I was enlightened I wouldn't be upset. There are no I shoulds or I shouldn'ts. There's no one here doing anything. Everything is just happening. I am the witnessing presence of whatever is happening. There's no more fighting with what is. There's no one here doing anything. There was never a separate entity here that did anything. There was just a belief in a separate entity here. That belief in a separate ego, a separate me, is at the root of all psychological suffering.

When there's no one here doing anything, there's just witnessing of whatever happens. It's the same as watching a movie on television. There's witnessing of this body/mind character called Stephen.

Darren: So you might be sad and just be watching that.

Stephen: There is sadness, and there's no sense that I shouldn't be sad. I need to meditate more. If I was enlightened I would always be happy—that's absurd! There is no one here who created the sadness. There's no one here who creates the happiness—it just happens, and it's witnessed.

Walter: That's a very good point you're making, and you're presenting it very well—the concept of being a witnessing presence. It's very good.

Stephen: Look in your own experience and you'll notice that this is the only thing you know with absolute certainty—that you are consciousness. Everything else can be debated—like the concepts of free will or destiny. You can believe there is free will or there isn't. But what can't be debated is that this witnessing presence *is*. It always is. It's just witnessing. There's always been this witnessing presence from the time you were a little child until right now. It's always now—now, now, now. So this is what I am. I am the eternal witnessing presence. I am eternal life. That's what I am.

Darren: Well, in my own experience, I cannot go beyond the time I became of aware of it. Before I was born I don't know if this awareness was there. I cannot speak about it. I have no sense of it.

Stephen: So we look and ask when does the sense of being separate happen? It didn't happen at one point in time. It happens every morning when you wake up. It happens throughout your day. The I-thought and image arises and falls. It arises in the morning with your story. As you're going about your day, taking care of your business, you become so involved in your work or whatever you're doing, the I-sense falls away.

Let's say you're a carpenter and you're completely involved in sanding a piece of wood, there's no I. The sense of I falls away, but what's always there? The consciousness, the witnessing presence is always there just watching. There's no suffering as the witnessing presence. And then someone shouts, Darren, get over here! Then the I image comes back in, and with it the potential for psychological suffering. Knowing yourself as this witnessing presence there's a new perspective.

Darren: So somebody could harm me, and I could respond by saying, that's not him harming me. He's just driven by consciousness.

Stephen: There is no separate entity.

Darren: No separate will or ego that can control matters.

Stephen: There is no separate entity in the universe at all. There's one universe. There's no way you could possibly separate yourself. Could you extract yourself from the rest of creation? Is that possible? And then exercise control—it's just not possible.

Darren: It's easy to fall for the belief in being a separate entity.

Stephen: That is the human experience. It's the fall from grace.

Darren: It's so easy to fall for that and feel that, oh, yeah, I can control my experience.

Stephen: Yes, and that's why there is psychological suffering.

The Master of man and his infinite Lover
He is close to our hearts, had we vision to see
We are blind with our pride and the pomp of our passions
We are bound in our thoughts where we hold ourselves free.
It is He in the sun who is ageless and deathless
And into the midnight His shadow is thrown
When darkness was blind and engulfed within darkness
He was seated within it immense and alone
—Sri Aurobindo

7

The Joy of No Me

Suzanne: In my own experience I'm finding that the attachment to certain desires seems to be dissolving. It's like I don't know what I want. I'm watching what's happening as the energy comes up, and I used to have very intense desires for things.

Stephen: What we really want is to feel a sense of peace and ease. A sense of acceptance, and the sense that everything is alright and okay the way it is. If everything works out the way we think it should and the way we want it to, what we want as an end result is to live in peace, and feel this sense of acceptance, this sense that everything's okay.

But we see it has nothing to do with whether or not we accomplish the things we want to accomplish or everything works out the way we want it to—whether it's our career, our personal lives, relationships, or financial goals. Whether or not things work out the way we think they should or not has nothing to do with what we really want from them. What we want is this peaceful sense of acceptance, the sense that everything is okay. And it turns out the peaceful sense of acceptance, the sense that everything is okay—is what we are. We *are* this peaceful sense of acceptance, the sense that everything is okay. And it has nothing to do with all the stuff.

So we just watch how everything turns out—the career, the relationships, the finances—all of that. We watch how it all turns out. We're just watching it, and there's a sense of peace, a sense of ease and acceptance of everything as it is. There's a sense of wonder—how is all of this happening, what's happening? I don't know! The peace comes through seeing we're not the I or the controller. We're not the character in the story who is trying to organize and fix our life situation and make sure it all turns out right.

We are the mystified clueless-ness that's watching the whole show and thinking, 'I don't know—I have no clue!' And there's a peaceful sense that everything is okay and all the stuff doesn't matter, you know. Because what I want out of it, if I get my life situation right is a peaceful sense of relaxation, and it turns out that's already here.

So whatever happens is just happening and there's a mystified clueless-ness watching it all. It's a peaceful sense of mystified clueless-ness. I'm using several different words because if we say consciousness or awareness, we already have concepts about them. But if we say this peaceful sense of mystified clueless-ness, you have to think and then, oh, yeah, that's what it is. This is what we are—it's our essence. It's this witnessing presence.

Suzanne: Another experience is I'm finding a lot of joy, I guess you'd call it, in very simple things. I mean, so many things in my day-to-day experience—a cup of tea and a cookie. Going for a walk with the dog with the sun in my face, or reading—it just goes on and on. It seems my moment-to-moment experience is bringing on a lot of joy, rather than looking to something big or something different than what's here now.

Stephen: When it's seen there's no me here, no ego, no controlling entity, what's left is this peaceful, mystified clueless-ness that's sort of floating around, and life is funny!

Whatever is happening, you're not doing any of it—you know that. Emotions come up and you feel, whoa! Where did that come from? That's my response to whatever comes up. Anger comes out of nowhere—what was that? I don't know where that came from. But there's no 'I should' or 'I shouldn't' response.

Suzanne: That is very liberating. There's a sense of freedom to be whatever comes out of you, and not judge yourself, hate yourself, or think you should have been different.

Stephen: Because there's no one there who did it. Whatever came up—there's no one there who did it.

Suzanne: Yes, it happened of its own.

Stephen: Everything is happening of its own.

Suzanne: That's my sense—it's all happening on its own. When I first read that everything was happening on its own, it didn't compute. It kept sticking and it really got my attention. Everything is happening of its own, which means there's no me doing anything. When it started to really sink in, I got it. Everything is happening spontaneously, it's all just happening and there's nothing I can do about it! You just have to let it happen, there's nothing to do. That's pretty much it.

Stephen: That's it. So, naturally, prior to seeing that, there's the sense that I am the doer, and there's the tension and resistance of being the doer. Seeing that there is no doer, naturally, all of that falls away. Because it's seen that I'm not doing anything, there's no me, everything is happening on its own. And the tension and resistance fall away. That's what we thought we were—the resistance. Things are this way, I want them another way—that's the resistance.

Suzanne: There was trying and struggling. I was just, oh my God—the monumental effort I was putting into things.

Stephen: When we see there's no one here doing anything, all the tension and resistance fall away. Whatever is coming up is coming from some mysterious source. There's no one here to resist anything. There's no one here who did anything. There's no one here to change anything. There's just the witnessing of it. There's just this peaceful, mystified clueless-ness.

Yes, there is a Nirvana; it is leading your sheep to a green pasture, and in putting your child to sleep, and in writing the last line of your poem.
—Kahlil Gibran

8

Awareness vs Consciousness

Julie: There is this essence, awareness. There's also a localization of awareness that is connected with this body, this character and conditioned responses. And there's a movement between the two. In the localization there's a sense of participation so there's still a duality going on. It feels like a dance.

So there's playing with the duality of localized awareness within the space of awareness. I don't know if the words I'm using to describe this you relate to at all, but I'm curious.

Stephen: Yes, I use the terms the way Nisargadatta uses them—awareness being the absolute. We will never experience awareness.

Julie: Right, it is what we are. Everything else is an object.

Stephen: Yes, and he uses the word *consciousness*, and that's when duality begins. So how do we know awareness exists? You can notice this in your own experience when you wake up in the morning and when you go to sleep at night.

When you wake up in the morning—Nisargadatta mentioned this in *I AM THAT*—he said you can watch yourself wake up, and watch yourself go to sleep. I thought, that's odd, and it passed. I didn't try to do it, but the next two mornings and evenings when I went to sleep, and woke up in the morning I noticed and knew what he was talking about. What happened was I was asleep and sunlight was coming through the window and shining into my eye, but at the time I wasn't conscious of that—I'm looking back now on the experience. The body was asleep so there was just awareness, there was nothing. There was nothing and everything. You can't say there's nothing, or you can't say there's everything—it's *absolutely nothing*. Then light came in and shined upon my eye, and upon awakening there was the thought 'I'. 'I' and that's it—only 'I'. First 'I' and then 'I sense sunlight.' It started with 'I...sense the sunlight.' So, now there's consciousness, duality. This 'I' is pure consciousness—'I'. It's complete peace. There are no problems. And then the story starts—I sense the sunlight, oh, what time is it? Is it time to go to work? Am I late? Did my alarm go off? I have to get to work. Today I have a presentation to do—this 'I' grows into 'me' and 'my' story.

Julie: The world gets constructed.

Stephen: Yes, the world, duality, consciousness—consciousness implies duality. As soon as the story started to develop, my eyes opened, I woke up and realized—oh, that's awareness! So then I recognized pure awareness, because at the moment the I-thought is born there has to be something watching the I-thought—it's pure awareness.

Then the story builds—I have to get up and go to work. I have responsibilities—this I-thought grows. But there has to be something witnessing that initial I-thought. There has to be something prior to consciousness, prior to 'I', prior to 'I am'. Otherwise what's witnessing it? What knows it? So this awareness *is*. It's our underlying essence, and you'll never experience it because as soon as you experience it it's dual and it's consciousness. That's the way I use the terms awareness and consciousness.

Jake: Is consciousness like thinking? Is consciousness different from awareness?

Stephen: They're the same in essence. But consciousness is relative, and awareness is absolute. This is conceptual and it's interesting to talk about, but it's not going to help you with psychological suffering. To be free of psychological suffering I'd stay with the practical aspects. Then you can talk about consciousness and awareness as concepts, and about all these interesting experiences.

So what am I? Am I this I-thought and the story, or was I there prior to that, and during that, and after that? You can make the same observation when you go to sleep. Your story is spinning in the head about everything that happened during the day, and what you have to do tomorrow. Then it slows down, slows down, slows down, and it goes down to—right before you fall asleep you'll notice there's just this sense of being, this consciousness, 'I'. The story is gone now as everything has settled down. There's just 'I'. And then even the 'I' is gone. But awareness is still there because if the alarm goes off...

Jake: There's something there that hears it.

Stephen: Yes, there's something there that hears it. We call that awareness or absolute awareness. It's absolute awareness because it's not relative to any particular experience or object.

Consciousness wakes up with 'I' and then the world and your story appear. So, what are you in essence? You are the absolute awareness. You can see consciousness wake up in the morning, and see it go to sleep at night. You only know awareness after the fact as a concept. You know it's there because something has to be there to witness the I-thought and the story appear—and then consciousness goes to sleep, but you know awareness is there because if the alarm goes off you'll hear it. So awareness, the absolute is there—you know it after the fact.

I tend to focus on the practical aspect because my interest in communicating this is to share the fact that it's possible to be free of psychological suffering and spiritual seeking. That's something you can live with and experience—it's tangible, palpable. It impacts your life experience—being free of suffering and seeking.

One with the Transcendent, calm, universal
Single and free, yet innumerably living
All in thyself and thyself in all dwelling
Act in the world with thy being beyond it.
Soul, exceed life's boundaries; Spirit, surpass the universe.
Outclimbing the summits of Nature
Transcending and uplifting the soul of the finite
Rise with the world in thy bosom
O Word gathered into the heart of the Ineffable.
One with the Eternal, live in His infinity
Drowned in the Absolute
—Sri Aurobindo

9

Mother Theresa and Charles Manson Happened

Stanley: Two people fighting—first of all there aren't two people. But there are two egos trying to control in some way. But they're not even in control of the fact that they're trying to control!

Stephen: It seems that everything is happening, doesn't it? Doesn't the weather happen? Thoughts happen. Pleasant, loving relationships happen. Unpleasant, unhealthy relationships happen. Everything is already happening, right?

Stanley: Yes.

Stephen: And there's a witnessing of it all. Mother Theresa was happening. Charles Manson was happening. There's no personal responsibility there. Obviously we want to put Charles Manson in prison; who wants to live with Charles Manson? If you had a chance to be with Mother Theresa that may have been a pleasant experience—I never met her. So that's all happening, but there's no personal blame of Charles Manson. But, at the same time, you want to separate him from society. I don't want Chuck hanging around us! He's a bit dangerous. But there's no personal blame. You know everything is happening, right? The earth is turning, the sun is shining, thoughts are happening. Love happens—hate happens.

Stanley: There seems to be a big dream machine—an incredible, unimaginably complex dream machine happening.

Stephen: It's pretty amazing.

We do act, and yet everything we do
Is God's creative action.
—Rumi

10

What Are You Going to Do About the Ego?

Stephen: Seeing in your own direct experience that there is no separate 'me' here doing anything—that's quite a blow to the ego, this 'me' that wants to control. What do you mean I'm not in control?

Jake: Can you talk about that a little bit, because I noticed there are still thoughts arising that imply I have influence, and I could have accomplished more at work today if I had gotten here earlier, or if I had...

Stephen: Well, maybe you could have accomplished more today, but it didn't happen that way. Notice in your own direct experience that I am this witnessing presence. This is what I am. I know this. This can't be denied or debated. I know this is my essence.

Now whether or not I can exercise control—if I had done X, then Y and Z would have happened—that's debatable, maybe it would have happened, maybe not. But is there any 'me' or 'I' there who can do it? And if so, what are you waiting for? Why don't you take control of your life right now?

We can see in our own direct experience everything is just happening. It's so obvious that the weather is just happening, and other things—our finger nails are growing. If your body is injured it will heal; you can't heal it, either it heals or it doesn't. Thoughts arise, feelings, it's all happening. There's no separate entity here doing any of it.

Even the sense of ego, the I should and shouldn't thoughts, the essence of the ego, the sense of control—these thoughts 'I should have done that' or 'I shouldn't.' Or even the thought 'I know better than that because I've seen clearly there is no separate controlling entity, no ego so I shouldn't be having these I should or shouldn't thoughts'—even that is just happening. So the sense of ego, the sense of being in control, you didn't create that—the ego sense.

Jake: Thank you.

Stephen: The ego sense just happens. The ego happens. Seeing clearly that even the sense of ego, the sense of me, and I am in control—even that just happens. That happens just like the weather. So you may have very clear periods of time when you're just floating along, there's no ego here, everything is happening, there's happiness, there's sadness, there's anger, everything is happening—it's clear. And then other times these ego thoughts and stories come in like, 'I know better than that now, I've seen the ultimate truth!' Even that is just happening. Those thoughts and the ego sense just happen. So that is witnessed— oh, there's that ego again! What are you going to do about it?

Jake: [laughing] That's great! Right there, what are you going to do about it? That's really good. I'm going to think a lot. That's what I usually do, and it doesn't work.

Stephen: Knowing this, seeing clearly there's no separate controlling entity here, it's just a story, it's just a belief—seeing this and knowing yourself as this consciousness, this witnessing presence, you take your stand, if you will, as this consciousness. I am this witnessing presence. I am watching the appearance of this ugly ego that arises at times. The ugliness of the ego arises. The selfishness, the selfish thoughts—it just happens. It's noticed, oh, there it is—it happens just like a weather storm happens.

In the secret cave of the heart, two are seated by life's fountain.
The separate ego drinks of the sweet and bitter stuff,
Liking the sweet, disliking the bitter.
While the supreme Self drinks sweet and bitter,
Neither liking this nor disliking that.
The ego gropes in darkness, while the Self lives in light.
—The Upanishads

11

The Sense of Ego is Free to Come and Go

Stephen: It can be quite common after it's recognized that awareness is what we are, everything is really peaceful for a while. Oh, okay, I get it. And then the ego sense, the sense of being in control comes back. Oh, no! I lost it! And then there's the sense that I have to do whatever I did before to get rid of the ego sense—but that's just more ego.

Jake: Right.

Stephen: So we see that I didn't create the ego, and I didn't get rid of the ego, the sense of being in control. That was gone for a while—I didn't get rid of it. I didn't create its re-appearance. So, even the ego is seen as just an appearance.

Sometimes the sense that I am in control comes into your experience—that ego sense comes back and expresses itself at work, in relationships—so that's witnessed. To get involved in trying to get rid of the ego is more ego. The ego was gone for a week or two and now it's back. Then the thought arises, I have to get rid of the ego. No, no, no, no! It's just the ego appearing, the sense of being in control. So, it's just witnessed—oh, there it is, and it passes on its own. Or it doesn't. It usually does if it's just witnessed.

Jake: Trying to get rid of it will make sure it stays.

Stephen: That's just it, yes. I'm finding that's common with folks. They're saying everything was fine for a while, just sort of floating around, everything was cool. Then the ego sense came back and it was very heavy. So now they're trying to get rid of it. No, no, no, don't try to get rid of it, just watch it. Because what you are in essence is this witnessing presence, this watching. All you can really do is witness. That's what you can do—witness.

Jake: And there's no failure when the ego sense re-appears, and that's what I heard tonight. It was a relief when you said that earlier. I was happy when you said that the ego sense comes and goes on its own.

Stephen: Yes, you never created the ego sense. You didn't get rid of the ego sense. It comes and goes on its own, just like the weather. Seeing that is quite liberating.

Jake: Exactly. When I think I screwed up because the ego sense is here...

Stephen: Yes, that's the same thing—the ego trying to get rid of the ego. The ego didn't create the ego, and the ego didn't get rid of the ego. Don't fight the ego. Let the ego go, just watch it.

Jake: Then I'm trying to figure, okay, what did I do that caused this to come up again. What was I saying? What was I thinking and how can I stop it?

Stephen: Yes, that's more of the same.

Jake: It's like, oh, I'm doomed! I've got the ego coming up. It's because I told that person this, and I shouldn't have done that.

Stephen: It's all the same process. That's pretty liberating—being free of fighting the ego. The ego is free to come and go. It always was anyway.

Jake: Right.

Stephen: Now it's recognized as just the ego. And the ego can be ugly.

Jake: It's the belief that my life would be better, the world would be better without my ego. And somehow it's my responsibility to take care of these things.

Stephen: It's pretty liberating to be free of the ego.

Jake: Very liberating—seeing the truth of it. That was my experience talking with you on the phone. It wasn't just concepts. I was finding the truth. You were putting out suggestions saying check this out, and that's what I was doing with you. I had these ideas I still believed, and I needed to look at them.

Stephen: You check in your own experience, and bite into the apple versus reading about it.

Jake: Yes, so this is very helpful to be able to look and ask, can I get rid of the ego? Did I make it show up? Can I get rid of it? I wasn't clear. I hadn't checked to the degree I have now with you here tonight. Earlier today I believed I was doing something wrong.

Let the dream unroll itself to its very end. You cannot help it. But you can look at the dream as a dream and refuse it the stamp of reality.
—Nisargadatta Maharaj

12

Get Clear On This

Stephen: Seeing the fundamentals of what I am, and what I am not cleared up the spiritual seeking and the psychological suffering, and put it into perspective. Once you know what you are, there's a different perspective on the stories and the images that are playing in the head. There's a new perspective. If you believe you are the character in the story that's playing in your head and that's who you are in essence, then you'll suffer along with the character. But when you see what you are in essence—not that you're not the character as a person, and we can talk about this—we can call it a person there who has relationships and thoughts and stories. And there's a body there, but that's not what you are in essence. But if you believe that I am this body and I am this person who is the central character in the story that's playing in the head, if this is who I believe I am, then I'll suffer along with the person, the image, the body and the stories—I'll suffer with that.

The spiritual literature points to the fact that we're not the body or the mind, you are consciousness—you are awareness, the witnessing presence, the Buddha mind, you are universal consciousness, you are life itself. You're not the body or the mind—the mind being the stories and the images. And you don't exist as a separate entity. You are an expression of the One. You are the One in essence.

What we are in essence is the same. We're all an expression of the One—whatever it is that created the universe is what we all are in essence. How could we possibly be separate? Is it possible for you to separate yourself from the rest of the universe, and then exercise control over the universe? Is it possible? It's not possible to be separate from the rest of the universe, and then exercise control. Whatever it is that is exercising control through you *is* the universal presence—whatever you want to call it, God, universal life itself.

All the spiritual literature, it seems to me, says the same thing—what you are in essence is life itself, you are consciousness or awareness, the witnessing presence—you are the One. Knowing yourself as the One in essence, the consciousness, there's a new perspective on the body and the mind, the stories, and the suffering me, the sense of ego, the sense of being in control, the sense of being separate from the rest of the universe.

If you feel you are separate from the rest of the universe then every moment of your life there's a certain degree of anxiety. Trying to get things right. Fighting against what you don't like, and trying to grasp on to what you do like; trying to avoid the negative, uncomfortable experiences, and trying to grasp on to the comfortable. So most every moment in your life there's an underlying sense of anxiety because I am separate from the universe and I have to exercise control over my experience. I always want to be happy, I never want to be sad. I always want to be successful, I never want to fail. I always want pleasure, I never want pain. The sense of being a separate entity creates the suffering. Because if I'm separate from the universe I always have to be on guard, I always have to be fighting and struggling to fix what's wrong and to hang on to what's right. So I'm always fighting.

Darren: Fighting for survival.

Stephen: Fighting for survival of the 'me' image. The body has a biological drive for survival, but there's no psychological suffering with that. If someone comes in here and attacks us we'll fight back. The organism will defend itself—or it won't. My interest in sharing this message is to share the fact that it's possible to be free of psychological suffering and it's possible to be finished with your spiritual search. That's my interest in sharing this message.

The reason I feel driven to share this is because for twenty some odd years I was suffering psychologically and looking for a way out. Reading books on psychology, philosophy, and then religious philosophy, Buddhism, Christian Mysticism, Zen and everything else—trying to get out of the suffering. There was a constant sense of anxiety and suffering and fighting with what is.

When my life situation worked out well, there was a sense that finally I got it right—for a while, for a few weeks, a few months, a few years, and then BOOM! It all got knocked out from under me. And I was right back into the psychological suffering. So it becomes obvious that getting your life situation in order isn't the source of peace, because it's a temporary experience.

Through the spiritual seeking we're told we can be free of suffering. When you stumble across the Eastern religious philosophies it's stated that if you recognize your true nature, find out who you are and realize what you are in essence is this consciousness, you'll be free of the psychological suffering, free of the ego, free of the sense of separation. So that becomes the goal. And we go to all the different

59

gurus around the country hoping to get some energy transfer and somehow be *zapped* into enlightenment.

I share from my own experience what helped me. All the religious philosophies seem the same to me in essence. Nisargadatta's words resonated with me and it just made sense to me. He's saying essentially the same thing the others are saying, and using his own terminology.

My interest in sharing this is to share the fact that it's possible to be free of seeking and suffering. It's really through two key insights, two points you see in your own direct experience. One is what you *are* in essence, and the other is seeing what you are *not*. It's stated that freedom from suffering comes when you see what you are in essence is this seeing, the witnessing, the consciousness, the awareness— whatever word works for you.

We can make the same observation we did last week to point to this because it's really effective. This is *tasting* what we are instead of reading about it. We know the concepts, but tasting this, taking the words off the page and biting into them changes your experience of what this consciousness is because now you know, oh, this is it!

If we look at this cell phone, we see it as an object. You see the colors, the lights, and the numbers. Notice the object, first of all, and now notice the *seeing* of the object—there's a *seeing*. There's an object and there's a *seeing* of the object. First, notice the object, then notice the *seeing* that's happening—seeing the object. Now we pick up a different object, a remote control, and we see this object. We see the different colors, and it's a different shape—now notice the *seeing*. There's a *seeing* of the object. The objects are different; they're different objects, but the *seeing*...

Darren: Is the same.

Stephen: It's the same. Any object—it doesn't matter. Notice the object, and notice the *seeing*. Now notice the thoughts that are arising in your head. Thoughts are arising, and there's a *seeing* of those thoughts. Now we hear some noises in the background, and we notice the hearing. Not just the sense of hearing, not just the sense of sight, but there is *awareness* of the sense of sight, there is awareness of the sense of hearing. And you can sense your body sitting here. There's awareness of the senses of the body. And again notice there is awareness of thoughts that are arising—there's a *seeing*. Whatever word you want to use—awareness or seeing.

60

Darren: An awareness of the awareness.

Stephen: We're noticing it.

Darren: Noticing the awareness.

Stephen: Yes, so instead of noticing the objects we notice the *seeing*. We can look at the object whether the object is a remote control, a cell phone, a thought or an image of you and your story. There's an image of you and your personal situation. The image of you and your personal situation is an object you're seeing. That image always changes. Sometimes the character is happy, sometimes sad. Sometimes successful, sometimes he fails. The object is always changing— different objects, different images. But the *seeing* is always the same.

So there's this consciousness, this seeing, this witnessing presence, this awareness—whatever word works for you. The words don't matter anymore because you know it, you've tasted it—it's no longer a concept. You're not reading about it in a book and wondering what is this consciousness? You've tasted this simple seeing. It watches the character as an image in your story that's playing—the happiness and sadness, laughter and the tears—all of that. There's a seeing of it. The objects of this *seeing* are constantly changing. The images, the stories, the feelings, the happiness, the sadness, and the body are always changing. Sometimes the body is healthy, and sometimes it's sick. There's a seeing of it, consciousness of it.

The spiritual literature, especially the Eastern spiritual literature, points to the fact that you are this consciousness, that's what we are in essence—this *seeing*. And knowing what you are *not*—you're not the image of yourself and your story. You're not the body, the body is always changing, it's healthy, then it's sick—it's young and it's getting older.

Your life situation is always changing—sometimes you have it all in order, and sometimes it's a complete mess, and sometimes it's half and half. But the seeing, the consciousness is always the same. It's just watching.

So it's seen that what I am is this witnessing, this consciousness. Everywhere I go—I get up and walk around, and everywhere I go I am this seeing. I'm just the seeing. It doesn't matter where I go.

Darren: Or sensing or hearing or whatever. You're just being aware of something being aware.

61

Stephen: Yes, awareness, consciousness. We can call it seeing—not the sense of sight but the awareness. Awareness takes it all in. So, use whatever word clicks for you. Some will say this *seeing*, but it encompasses all of it, everything. What I am in essence is this consciousness, and everything comes and goes through this consciousness. The thought-stories when you wake up in the morning—there's a period of time when there's just consciousness or the seeing before the image of you and your story comes in. So you notice that when there's just the seeing, there's no psychological suffering. And you notice that psychological suffering begins when your self image appears—just like an object—your self image is just like this bottle, it's no different. It's an appearance in you, consciousness. It's an appearance in the seeing—this self image.

If there's a belief that I am this image, this separate entity—if I am that image, then there's going to be suffering. There will be swings in our experience. Because we think we are that image. But when it's pointed out that what you are is this witnessing presence, you are the seeing, you are the watching, then you just watch these crazy stories that are playing and wonder, where do they come from? They just appear—you didn't create the images. Sometimes the images are disturbing.

So we just notice that what I am is this witnessing presence. I am this consciousness, then we watch the story. We watch the appearance of our self image and the whole story. It may be spinning out of control and very uncomfortable with all sorts of problems—personal issues, relationship issues, financial problems, physical health—the whole thing. It's just a story spinning. It's just images, it's just an object in me, and I am the *awareness* of it.

Knowing yourself as the witnessing presence, the consciousness, the seeing—you watch. And whatever stories present themselves are witnessed. Sometimes the stories will be pleasant, sometimes unpleasant, but you are the witnessing presence of the stories.

You're not trying to do anything about the story, you're just watching the stories and you're noticing that I am the witnessing and I am watching this story. To get involved in the stories and try to fix them, we're playing in the dream, playing in the imagination, and looking for a way out.

There's a dream happening, and in the dream the central character is trying to get out of the dream story. Trying to get out of the dream is part of the dream.

13

I Am Consciousness—So What?

Jason: Over the past couple of weeks what I've experienced is the clarity that everything is happening in consciousness, this awareness. But there's still been identification with the story, and there's still been psychological suffering. I'm not expecting a bang, poof, I'm consciousness, okay, bye, that's the end of it. I've been reading John Wheeler's book, and there's a quote from Nisargadatta about the ending of psychological suffering.

Should I put a little more attention on the *seeing*, is that it? You know, to relieve the psychological suffering. To realize I'm not the character in the story. I know I'm not that, but the story is still playing, and I'm identifying with it because I can feel it in my body, and it feels very real. When imagination comes on, I'm suffering over stories that are not even real, and it's ridiculous. I'm seeing this, and it's ridiculous, but I'm still suffering over it.

Darren: I love what Jason just said because it's one thing to have an intellectual understanding that who I really am is the One consciousness looking through these eyes. But there's a distinction between that and being established in that to the point that nothing matters really. Being so clearly in that, you know, things could happen, and you say, well that's just stuff happening—okay. What I'd like to be able to do is get beyond the intellectual understanding that I am That, and really get that I am That.

Stephen: Okay, let's look at that, and we want to address the psychological suffering. The seeing of what you are is not intellectual. You are that. If you see this object, [holding up a bottle] notice the *seeing*.

Darren: Right.

Stephen: Notice the seeing. Just notice the seeing right now. The seeing is happening, this consciousness.

Darren: Right.

Stephen: There's consciousness of your body sitting there, and other bodies here. In your peripheral vision you can see other things in consciousness. Everything comes and goes in this.

Darren: Right.

Stephen: Even the thought and the word you just spoke, "right," comes and goes in this. So this is not intellectual.

Darren: Well, maybe it's not intellectual, but it's not established in a way that...

Stephen: There's nothing to be established in. See this object here? [holding up a cell phone]

Darren: Yes.

Stephen: Are you noticing the consciousness? Everything is in this consciousness right now. This is not intellectual—this consciousness. There's nothing to be established in. You can't get out of this consciousness. Everywhere you go the consciousness goes, too. This is not an intellectual understanding of consciousness.

Darren: So if it's not intellectual, then what is it?

Stephen: It's an experiential recognition. What is this consciousness? It just *is*. It's non-conceptual, isn't it? There's an awareness of the words I'm speaking right now. Is the awareness of these words, the awareness that's here right now—it's always here right now, right now, now, now—is it conceptual?

Darren: No, it's awareness.

Stephen: Okay, that's it. This is what we are. Now a concept can arise, "Yes, but what is this awareness, what is consciousness?" And that also happens in this awareness. Concepts arise just like any other object. The word 'awareness' arises. Consciousness is this *seeing*.

Darren: But then the question that comes up for me always is, "So what?" So now I am this consciousness!

Stephen: Okay, this consciousness is what we are. What you are is, "So, what!" There's no problem with it. We're all sitting here and there's consciousness of whatever happens—so what? There's no suffering as this consciousness!

When does psychological suffering happen, when does it begin? It begins when there's a belief that I exist as a separate, controlling entity, a separate person. If there's belief in the existence of this separate entity, there will be suffering.

At the root of all psychological suffering is this me image, this I. I exist as a separate, controlling entity, and the story revolves around this me image. This me has relationships, this me has finances, this me has a career, this me has feelings and sensations. This me has power and it has to *exercise* its power over its experience. It has to exercise power over relationships, finances, career, feelings, sensations, and actions. If there's a belief that this I, or this me exists as a separate, controlling entity then there will be psychological suffering.

But if we see that I am not this me image and there's no one here who created this me image and the stories—they're just appearing in consciousness somehow. Like everything else appears in consciousness—trees, birds, dogs and cats, people, this room, and all the other objects that appear in awareness. There's no separate controlling entity here. Why doesn't a bottle of water have psychological suffering? Because it doesn't have the capacity for self-reflection or the creation of this I-image, this me—I exist as a separate entity—"you better not drink me!"

Darren: Do animals have that sense of I?

Stephen: I don't think they have psychological suffering, but that's speculation. I know in my own direct experience, and we can all look in our own direct experience, and we can see—when does psychological suffering begin? It begins when there's belief that I exist as a separate entity—a separate, controlling entity. I have my own separate power and I'm able to exercise my power over thoughts. I can exercise power over feelings, sensations, and images. And I'm able to control my experience so I'll always be happy and successful.

But what if we look in our own direct experience and see, well, what is this me that I think I am? Who's in control? Is there anyone here who's in control, or is everything just happening?

Darren: Well, it seems so enticing to believe, yes, I do have control. As an individual I do have some control. I drove my car here, you know. Or at least that seems very clear to me.

Stephen: If there's a belief in a separate I, and I exist as a separate, controlling entity who is able to exercise control over its experience—do you see how that's at the root of psychological suffering? And how all psychological suffering revolves around this image of me?

When there's no self-image, no story playing in the head, there's no psychological suffering! It's only when the me image comes in. Psychological suffering is relative to me at the center—and my relationships, my career, my finances—me—it's me at the center. When there's no me thought, no me image, no I thought, or I image—which is just an image—when there's no me image, there's no psychological suffering!

If you're watching the baseball game, there's no I image involved, you're just watching the game. You want your team to win, but if they lose, you're not suffering psychologically. At the root of psychological suffering is the unexamined belief that I exist as a separate controlling entity who is able to exercise control over thoughts, feelings, sensations, relationships, actions, career, and finances—your whole experience. We can see the only time that you're suffering psychologically is when this me image appears and it's believed to be what you are in essence.

Jason: That's what I experience and it seems to have a life of its own. Okay, I know I am the seeing, but for some reason I get caught up in my story. Maybe because my life situation now is particularly intense—it just grabs me. Even when my experience is the densest, the most contracted—the clarity of seeing is just so perfectly clear—it's still like glass, but there's still the psychological suffering. So I want to know if this is a transition, or should I do something or not do anything?

Stephen: Is there anyone there in your experience who can change those images? Is there any separate controlling entity called 'me' who creates the images and the stories that spin? Is there anyone who's creating them that you can find and say, this is me creating these images? Or are the images and stories just happening?

66

Jason: I think it starts with the sense of 'I' as a separate entity, and then I have to protect this image. I have to make sure this image survives on all these different levels. It starts off with the sense of I, and then it grows beyond that. It seems to have a life of its own.

Maybe this is part of the process, you know. John Wheeler spent some time with Bob Adamson. You spent some time with John, and it wasn't like it was clear in ten minutes. I think Nisargadatta said it takes about a week of really being pointed out. And even John says in his book, generally people don't get it from books. I've been reading books for eons, and I got more from the last time we spent together than I did from reading stacks of hundreds or thousands of dollars I spent on books. Because it's been all concepts until now, but there's still some energy keeping the stories going.

Stephen: Is there anyone there doing that—creating the stories and the images, the I-thought, the images of being a person, and the story and the suffering that involves, or is all of that just happening?

Jason: It's just happening.

Stephen: And you see it.

Jason: I see it.

Stephen: Yes. That's it. There's nothing to do.

Jason: I'm seeing the story, but I'm becoming identified with it because I'm experiencing anxiety, and I experience fear. It's just happens. I don't want it to happen. I can partially see that it's just happening in consciousness, but I read that the acid test is when experientially you're free of psychological suffering. I know I'm still to some degree suffering psychologically over this me image. I don't know if maybe it burns itself out, or noticing the seeing lessens the power of it. That's it, I don't know if I'm expressing myself clearly.

Stephen: You are, very clearly. What's actually suffering when the suffering is happening?

Jason: It's the body, the body.

Stephen: The body suffers.

Jason: Yes.

Stephen: It's an uncomfortable energy in the body.

Jason: It's an uncomfortable energy in the body, yes.

Stephen: So there's discomfort in the body, the stomach is churning, there's tension in the neck and chest, or wherever it might be.

Jason: It's a physical sensation.

Stephen: So the body suffers.

Jason: Right. There's no pain in the brain.

Stephen: There's no psychological entity who suffers. The image you have of yourself doesn't suffer.

Jason: No, it's the body that's suffering.

Stephen: Yes, that's the only thing that can suffer.

Jason: I've come to that conclusion. I've seen that myself the past two weeks. The brain doesn't suffer, it doesn't feel anything. It's the body. That's where I'm experiencing the suffering—in my body.

Stephen: Yes, the body suffers. There's no personal entity there suffering.

Jason: No, just the body.

Stephen: There's no psychological entity there who can suffer. There is actually no such thing as psychological suffering.

Jason: Right. It's the body that's suffering.

Darren: But how can you say that? If you've ever been depressed that's psychological suffering, right?

Jason: You feel it in the body.

Stephen: There's no psychological entity who can suffer. Can an image suffer? The only thing that can suffer is the body.

Darren: Okay.

Stephen: We call it psychological suffering because at the root of it there's an image of me, an 'I' being separate who has to take control of its life. So there's a story playing. It's the same as watching a horror movie—fear can arise, anticipation, what's going to happen? Is someone going to get killed? So there's a story playing in the head. The body gets tense, the stomach churns—the body experiences that.

But there is no psychological entity that suffers. It's a story. Even the story I tell that I was suffering for twenty years is not true. Only this body was experiencing uncomfortable energy. Saying I was suffering psychologically is just a story, an image of myself, and then saying I was suffering. There is no psychological suffering.

Jason: I agree with you. It's the body that suffers. So is there anything to be done about the images causing the body to suffer?

Stephen: Is there anyone there? Can you find a separate, controlling entity who's creating the images and the story, or are they just appearing, just happening? Or, as you said, the stories have a life of their own?

Jason: Well, I react to certain things that happen and then it brings in the I image—I this and I that, then it just goes on its own. When we say psychological suffering, we can only feel psychological pain in the body. You get nervous, or you get calm—it's in the body so that's where I experience it.

Stephen: There is no separate entity. If you look in your own direct experience for this 'me', all you can find is a series of stories and images. You may feel the sense of being in control—you can feel it, but you can't find it.

Jason: It's just like you say—you can feel it, but you can't find it.

Stephen: If you feel like you are in control, look at your thoughts— can you control thoughts?

Jason: I wouldn't be thinking the thoughts I had if I was in control.

Stephen: Okay, so thoughts just arise.

Darren: Some thoughts you have control over.

Stephen: Oh, no you don't.

Darren: Well, when it comes to practical things, I think I've got to do this, I've got to do that.

Stephen: There's no one there. Stay with this.

Darren: Okay.

Stephen: It's not that thoughts and actions don't happen, but there's no one there doing them.

Darren: Okay.

Stephen: Let's look and find out if there is someone there doing it. We're not just going to believe it. That doesn't do any good. And we can simply reject it, get in the car and go home. But if you look in your own direct experience and say, well, I want to look into this sense of being in control, because the sense of being separate and in control is at the root of psychological suffering. When you see there's no one here in control, there's an absolute surrender.

So let's look in our own experience. Is there any entity there who controls thoughts or do thoughts just arise?

Jason: They seem to arise. Sometimes there's a feeling that they're *my* thoughts, but I certainly don't have control over them. Some of the thoughts are repetitive so they become familiar. But I can't exercise control over them, because if I could I would just say that when I get up tomorrow morning I'm going to have only the best thoughts, and the best feelings, the best sensations, and the best actions.

Darren: But to some degree he could do that, right?

Stephen: No.

Jason: I've been trying.

Stephen: Check in your own experience. If you believe you are in control of your thoughts, make that belief practical. Go ahead and exercise control of your thoughts. Do it now. Why are you waiting?

Darren: Well, I can say that when I'm driving home tonight I can think about this, that or the other.

Stephen: Thoughts just arise.

Darren: Okay, so the thought to think about something in particular just arose. So when I get in the car, I said that I would think about that.

Stephen: Maybe you will, maybe you won't. Watch in your own experience. See if there is any separate, controlling entity creating thoughts, or do thoughts just appear. And actions happen or they don't. Is there an entity there who creates thoughts?

Darren: Well, thoughts just pop into your head, but my question is, is there any exception to that? When it looks like a thought just popped into my head, but it was something that I planned, it was a contrived thing—like, okay, I'm going to do this?

Stephen: Check in your own experience and you can answer that question. And then it won't be a matter of someone telling you, or believing or not believing.

Darren: For example, I can say that when I'm driving home tonight I will think about this question, and when I'm driving home I'll think about this question. It's a conscious decision. You could say the conscious decision itself came from somewhere else, and it makes it look like it was my decision—I can buy that. So ultimately it all boils down to the fact that you have no control at all.

The body, heaven and hell, bondage and liberation, and fear too, all this is pure imagination. What is there left to do for me whose very nature is consciousness? —**Ashtavakra Gita**

14

The Pit Bull is Dead!

Stephen: It doesn't matter what's happening. It doesn't matter if an uncomfortable story is playing in the head—I'm still the *seeing*. The story passes, I'm still the seeing. The baseball game is on, I'm still the seeing. The game is over, I'm still the seeing. I go to sleep and wake up—the seeing is here. The stories start playing again, the seeing is still here, this consciousness. So what am I in essence? Am I the story, the image—or am I this consciousness?

Jason: Well, the seeing, the seeing. I mean, it's quite clear. When this is really seen and understood, I imagine the belief in my story is seen as just arising, and there's nobody here, then the body should stop reacting to it, or maybe not—I don't know.

Stephen: Is there any separate entity there creating the images?

Jason: No.

Stephen: Or the thoughts?

Jason: No.

Stephen: Or the feelings, the uncomfortable sensations in the body?

Jason: No.

Stephen: It's just happening. There's no one doing it.

Jason: There seems to be a relationship between the thoughts and the uncomfortable sensations.

Stephen: Right. Where do the thoughts come from?

Jason: [shrugging shoulders]

Stephen: Right, that's it.

Jason: And all the suffering is because of the futility of trying control.

Stephen: Yes, if there's a belief that I can somehow do something about these images—the I-image and the story generating this uncomfortable energy in the body, if there's the sense that I need to do something about the images, it's just more of the same suffering.

Jason: I've been banging a hammer against an iron wall for a long time. That's what it feels like.

Stephen: So the question comes up—okay, I see that I am this consciousness, this seeing...

Jason: I know that. That I have seen.

Stephen: The story is still playing, and the story is affecting the physical body. Then the thoughts arise, 'Shouldn't this be different? Is it a matter of time? I read that it could take time.'

Jason: Yeah, should I do affirmations to change my thoughts? Do I need to take medication to relax my body? Or maybe I should drink more! I don't know!

Stephen: Yes, that's all the same. There's a belief that there's some separate, controlling entity there who can do something about the images. So it's seen there's no one here who can do anything. If you don't believe that, then go ahead and take control—which you've already done for twenty or thirty years.

Jason: Yeah.

Stephen: You've already tried that for twenty or thirty years. That is at the root of psychological suffering—the belief that I exist as a separate, controlling entity who can exercise control over my thoughts, my feelings, my sensations, my actions, my experience. I am a separate controlling entity—that is at the root of suffering. So this is seen clearly—the suggestion is to check and see in your own experience, what are you in essence? Are you this consciousness? And you see, well, yes, I'm always this. So you see that.

And the assumption is now the stories should go away, and I should have a different experience. What should I do to change the story so

73

the body doesn't suffer? What should you do?—what you *are*. You are this witnessing presence, so you witness, you watch.

Any doing or attempt to change things is more of the same. It's what you've already done for twenty or thirty years. It may be uncomfortable, but any attempt to change or do anything about it is more of the same. Even the attempt to accept it and say, oh, I should accept this—no, no, no! Or I should try to avoid it. That's just more of this sense that I'm in control. There's not a damn thing you can do about anything at all, and there never was.

Darren: So what do you do?

Stephen: What you *are*. You can do what you are. You are this witnessing presence.

Darren: Okay, so how do you *do* what you *are*?

Stephen: You don't have to—there's nothing to do. How do you *do* consciousness? The seeing happens. The hearing happens. Everything is happening. Consciousness is already happening. It doesn't matter what happens in consciousness. Consciousness is already happening. You can't un-do it. Try not to do consciousness. It's like being told to stay in the present moment, stay in the here and now. You can't get out of the here and now. What do you do to stay in the present moment? Try to get out of it!

There's no doing. This is what's meant when you read in non-duality books that there's nothing to do, nothing can be done, and it's disturbing. There were times that would annoy me when I'd read there's nothing you can do. Because I wanted to do something, but that wanting to do something *is* the very suffering. The assumption of wanting to do something is that there's a separate, controlling entity here who can exercise control. So we look and observe in our own experience, and we see there is no separate controlling entity— thoughts just arise, feelings, sensations, actions—they're all just coming into consciousness.

So a natural surrendering happens. It's not the surrendering of 'I surrender.' It's seeing that you were fighting a war your whole life with an unloaded weapon. This 'me' this 'I' has no power. So a surrendering happens. Your whole life you've been fighting and battling what is—with an unloaded weapon!

74

There is no separate power here. Whatever is happening, is happening. Just like the weather happens—thoughts happen, and stories happen when you wake up in the morning. So what can you do? You can witness, watch, see—because that's what you are. You are this witnessing, and you can witness the discomfort in the body, but there's not a damn thing you can do about anything.

If there's an uncomfortable energy in the body and you want to burn it off, you can go for a walk. There are physical things you can do if you wake up and the story is playing in the head. You know it's just a story, and I am the witnessing of it, but the story is still playing and it creates an uncomfortable energy in the body. So you go for a walk to burn off the energy.

But you know there's no one there to do anything about the story, and the images—you can't get rid of them. They just appear and spin, and the body is uncomfortable and irritated. So you go for a walk to burn off that energy. But there's no one there to do anything about the images, the thoughts, feelings, and sensations—they just arise. There's no separate, controlling entity there. So you say, the hell with this, I'm going for a walk! The story is spinning so you go for a walk and burn off the energy.

Jason: John Wheeler mentions in his book that he reached a point where he doesn't pay much attention to thoughts anymore.

Darren: To what?

Jason: He doesn't pay much attention to his thoughts whatever they are anymore.

Stephen: Right, because they're all meaningless.

Jason: Right, so obviously I've been giving tremendous meaning to my thoughts. As the story has less meaning, I assume there will be less disturbing sensations, because the thoughts are seen to be untrue. The only reason I have disturbing sensations in my body is because I believe my thoughts and stories are true.

Stephen: Right.

Jason: If I really see that my thoughts and stories are not true I wouldn't suffer.

75

Stephen: These stories have been playing for a long time, and there's been belief in the stories. This is very common—let's say you've been working at the same company for twenty years, and you get on the highway and drive north everyday for twenty years. Then your company moves to the south.

You've been going north for twenty years. You start to drive to your new workplace the first day, and you drive north! You know your workplace has moved to the south, but it's the habit of the mind, the way it works. Do you beat yourself up for driving north, or do you just realize it's the nature of the mind and the habits that were formed over twenty years?

So if you wake up in the morning and the uncomfortable story is still playing, you just watch it. You don't beat yourself up over it and say, I should know better by now. I've seen clearly that I am this simple presence of awareness so I shouldn't be having these stories anymore, and the body shouldn't be affected. You've been driving north for twenty years! You know you don't work up north anymore; you know you work to the south. It's just a natural habit, the way the mind works. So you see it and you say, oh, it happened again I drove north! You turn around and you drive south. You don't beat yourself up over it, and go back to the spiritual seeking, and say, oh, I have to meditate more, I never really understood this, what's wrong with me? A friend of mine changed work location and he goes south right away.

There may be a time when the stories just happen, and you say, oh, there's the story again! If the story is causing disturbing sensations, you go for a walk to burn off the uncomfortable energy.

Jason: Or go to the gym.

Stephen: Yes, but there's nothing you can do about the story or the thoughts—everything's just happening. Some people may drive south immediately. Some people may take years for the habit to pass. But you're not suffering over it. You notice it and say, there go the thoughts again. What am I going to do about it? If you drive north, you say, here I go again!

Jason: If the thoughts are not believed, there's not going to be the reaction in the body. From my experience, it's only when the thoughts are believed that they affect me. I can have the thought that I'm a millionaire, but I don't feel like a millionaire!

76

Stephen: Right. You know what though?—if you walked down the street where you live everyday for twenty years and there was a pit bull that came out and bit you, you'd be conditioned to respond. So every day for twenty years a pit bull bit you, then the pit bull dies. And the owner gets a miniature dachshund to replace it. So for twenty years you've been getting bit by a pit bull, and now you walk by the house and hear the little dachshund growl—there will be a disturbing response in your body.

Jason: It's the conditioning.

Stephen: Even though you know the pit bull is dead! What do you do? You watch and say, oh, there's that disturbing response!

Jason: Okay.

Stephen: You're not creating the response. It's just happening. You know the pit bull is dead. You don't believe the pit bull came back to life! You know there's a miniature dachshund there now that couldn't bite its own toe nail off, but there's a conditioned response. You don't have to suffer over it, you just notice the response. You know it's a miniature dachshund. You don't beat yourself up over it, and say, oh, if I really believed this, try to focus in and really believe that the pit bull is dead.

Jason: I've been experiencing the absolute clarity. Even in the density of everything happening there is this pure seeing. So that's what's been happening—the conditioning.

Stephen: You've been driving north-bound for twenty years!

Jason: It's just this conditioning. I expect with more seeing, identification with the stories loses its power.

Stephen: You've been driving north-bound for twenty years. After a certain period of time you'll automatically drive south bound. It's the same with walking down the street and getting bit by a pit bull everyday for twenty years.

Jason: It could be a week or a month or a year.

Stephen: It may be a few days, it may be a month—but you know you've seen clearly that the pit bull is dead! You've seen clearly that you are this witnessing presence. You've seen clearly you are not the images and the stories. There's nothing to do. You don't have to do anything else. You've seen it clearly. The habit and conditioning of twenty years may come up for a while—a few days, months, years—who knows?

Jason: I don't know.

Stephen: It could go in a snap. You don't have to suffer over it, or try to get rid of it, and say, what's wrong with me? Where are my books? I have to go to more retreats and seminars!

Everything is happening. Even the conditioning is happening. We don't create our conditioning. We don't create anything—everything just happens.

Although you arrived in the world with nothing but the Unborn Buddha-mind, you fell into your deluded ways as you were growing up by watching and listening to other people in their delusion. You picked up all this gradually over a long period of time, habituating your mind to it. But none of your deluded thoughts is inborn. They cease to exist in a mind that's affirming the Unborn.

Illusory thoughts, if you just let them come and let them go away, one day you'll find they've vanished into the Unborn Buddha-mind.
—Zen Master Bankei

15

The Puppets and the Puppeteer Are One

Darren: When a thought comes up that I'm going to be doing this or that, it's my idea, it's me, me, me—the practical thing to do at that time is to say, well, maybe that's not true? There's something else driving all these thoughts?

Stephen: We can look right now. Where do thoughts come from? I don' know! It seems so obvious. Is there anyone in control? Look now. Is there anyone in control, or does the next thought just arise? What's your next thought going to be?

Darren: I cannot predict what it's going to be, right.

Stephen: No, there's no way to know. And what's your response to that next thought going to be? You can't predict what thought is going to arise. It just pops in and there it is.

Darren: And even the response is unpredictable.

Stephen: Yes, what's your response to the thought going to be?

Darren: It's unpredictable. I'm trying to see if I can draw a parallel between this and being an actor on stage going through all the drama, but being fully conscious of the fact that he's not the person he's playing.

Stephen: It's all happening, right. The person is happening.

Darren: But the One that is making all that happen...

Stephen: Is a mystery.

Darren: He's not the one the audience sees. He could be playing a villain, but actually he's a saint.

Stephen: Yes, a good analogy is the puppet and puppeteer. Not that we're puppets, it's just an analogy, because we're not separate. The analogy is that we are all puppets here—puppets are made of cloth, plastic, string and other material. So there's no separate control here.

There's a puppeteer controlling the show. The puppeteer is the mysterious source of all existence. What's moving these puppets is a mystery. There's nothing here but puppets. There's a mysterious source—what's the source of the universe? It's a mystery isn't it? Where does the universe come from?

Darren: You're saying we are *that*—we are the source.

Stephen: There's no separation. Only when thought comes in is there the appearance of separation. There's no separate God—no separate human. There's no such thing as the spiritual world, or the physical world until a thought comes in. It's all one movement until thought comes in.

There's no separate puppet, there's no separate puppeteer or source—the source over here, moving the puppet over there. It's just an effective analogy or metaphor to look and see that these bodies are like puppets. There's nothing that is not God. There is no human over here and God out there.

Darren: The puppet and the puppeteer are...

Stephen: One—and all the puppets. It's all one movement. How can it be different? How can it be separate? Is it possible for one entity to separate itself from the rest of creation and then exercise control over it?

Darren: If we use the word God—even God cannot separate himself from his creation.

Stephen: No, it's all one movement. As soon as thought comes in there's the appearance of separation. If *everything* in the universe is green, *everything*—is there any such thing as green? If *all* is green, there's no such thing as green.

If *everything* in the universe is God, it's all one—is there any such thing as God? We're just playing with words, but it puts these words and concepts into perspective. There is no God over here, and human beings over there. There's no separate me over here creating my thoughts, and God over there creating all human thoughts. It's just one movement.

16

Magical Powers and More Enlightenment Myths

Stephen: There's this seeing, this consciousness, and you notice the characteristics of this—are there any problems with this? No, it's just this *seeing*.

Jason: It's clear. It's transparent. It's clean.

Stephen: There's no problem with it, and this is what I am. My interest in sharing this message is to share the fact that it's possible to be free of suffering and spiritual seeking.

I'm not interested in parting the Red Sea, healing the sick, or making the blind see. Maybe that happens, but there's no one doing it. If we're caught up in thinking that I can attain enlightenment and I'll be able to wave my hand and transfer energy, or I'll be able to heal the sick and make gold nuggets manifest—there's no one doing that. If we think that if I have this understanding, or enlightenment, or awakening or whatever, I'll get special powers; that's more of the same old bullshit—trying to take control!

Jesus didn't say, I am the healer—he said, I and the Father are one. I can of my own self do nothing. I can of my own self do nothing! You who see me see the Father. When they came to him and praised him he said, why do you call me good? There is one who is good that is God. Because he realized they were looking to him personally as a separate entity. I and the Father are one. I am. I am the way, the truth and the life. This I Am—this seeing, this sense of being, this consciousness, this life. If there are any powers or abilities that happen, fine. There's no one doing it. If there's any credit taken—like come to me, I'm the healer—that's nonsense!

Darren: I'm just realizing that Jesus was perhaps one of the first non-dualist, right? He said, I and the Father are One.

Stephen: Well, there were others in the East and the West. And Moses said that God is the I AM THAT I AM. It seems to me that all of the ancient traditions and religious philosophies point to the same fundamental truth—there is no separate entity, there's just this consciousness, God, awareness, this seeing, or whatever word we use.

There is no separate entity here. We can say I am this is-ness, this sense of being, this seeing—call it I Am. I am the way, the truth, and the life. No one can come to the Father, but by me—I Am—not Jesus. He didn't say by me personally—I Am.

Jason: That was misunderstood.

Stephen: Yes, this I am. All of us can say, I am, it's the same I am. I and the Father are one. I am the way, the truth and the life. No one can come to the Father, but by me, I am. I am the door—I am.

Darren: Is he saying you can reach the Father through the understanding that all there is, is the seeing, experiencing.

Stephen: It seems to me that when it's realized that there's no separate person here who can do anything, there's just this consciousness, this seeing, this witnessing presence—you're done. There's nothing more to search for, there's no more seeking. You can seek after experiences, powers, abilities, or the admiration of others because you're such an enlightened being and you can transfer powers—that's just more of the same old crap. There's no difference between that and Donald Trump, and there's nothing wrong with Donald Trump. I'm not saying there is. That's just seeking after money, power and fame. Now I want money, power and fame because I can transfer energy and I'm special. Not that there's anything wrong with any of that.

Darren: Let's say, for example, suddenly you discover that the puppet you are can do magic, transfer power or whatever. You say, hey, this puppet can make money or become famous doing that. So, why not? I'll do it!

Stephen: Yes, that happens.

Darren: As long as you recognize you are just a puppet—and the puppeteer.

Stephen: Everything is happening. Nothing matters anyway. It really doesn't matter. It doesn't matter what you do. To whom does it matter? Eventually we'll be gone anyway. The sun will burn out, the planet will be gone. Ultimately what difference does it make?

Darren: Then the question becomes what does one do? Just wait to see what the next signal from the puppeteer is and work it out?

Stephen: The doing is already happening, but you're not the doer. Whatever's going to be done is going to be done. Who's doing it? Witnessing is happening, this watching—and it's pretty amazing—what's going on?

Darren: I'm glad you insisted on saying what it is you want to share because this is the first time I have become as clear as I have become. I heard something like this from Wayne Liquorman who said, you may be the doer of your actions, but you are not the author of your actions. And I felt, wow, that's interesting. But it just got very clear and deeper tonight. Thanks.

Little Lamb, who make thee?
Dost thou know who made thee?
Gave thee life, and bid thee feed
By the stream and o'er the mead;
Gave thee clothing of delight,
Softest clothing, woolly, bright;
Gave thee such a tender voice,
Making all the vales rejoice?
Little Lamb, who made thee?
Dost thou know who made thee?
—William Blake

What Happened When You Finally Got It?

Darren: One last question. When you got it, finally got it clear—was it like a euphoric experience or was it like a non-event? Like, oh, that's what it is, alright.

Stephen: No, it's just clear seeing. All of the psychological suffering is imaginary. This I, this me character is imaginary. There is no separate, controlling entity—all there is, is this consciousness. So there's the recognition that I am this consciousness. I've always been this consciousness, so it's nothing new. It's not a new state. It's not a new thing you've attained.

It's a recognition of what's always been here, this witnessing, this consciousness. This consciousness has always been here. The seeing has always been here. And now it's seen that the imaginary character, Stephen, who I felt I was—a separate, controlling entity who was responsible for controlling thoughts, feelings, and my life experience—that was seen to be non-existent. It doesn't exist.

It's noticed that I am this witnessing presence and everything is just happening. So there's nothing to do.

From within or from behind, a light shines through us upon things and makes us aware that we are nothing, but the light is all.
—**Ralph Waldo Emerson**

Practices to Do?

Jason: When you point to consciousness using different objects—the cell phone and the remote control—I really get a taste of the seeing. For the past couple of weeks I really haven't been thinking about this much. Occasionally I say, oh, yeah, I am the seeing. Or I'll contemplate not being an individual.

I'm not asking for a practice, but is it worth sitting for a moment and slowing down, rather than being totally engulfed in thoughts? Even though the seeing is still here, it seems to be contracted or focused on this one thought-story. It's more open and expansive when I'm noticing the seeing.

Can you suggest relaxing back into that, or maybe doing a little inquiry? Right now I know I am the seeing, but there's still the sense of being an individual. I don't know if it's waning. Maybe it happens so slow in the brain or however it happens. That's something I'm contemplating—is there an individual here?

There's always a sense of self, and the self gets identified with the thought-story, and it's all just happening. But I don't know if it's a legitimate question because the thought-story is still being seen. I'll think, well, it's happening in consciousness, and it's being seen, so...

Stephen: There's really nothing to do. Anything you do, you're right back into the same old game. That's not being dogmatic about non-duality, and saying there's nothing to do—there's really nothing to do! If I stop and ask, is there anything to do? As soon as the thought and feeling come up of doing something, that's the resistance. Trying to do something is the problem!

Jason: My sense of doing and seeking has really gone by the wayside. I know it's already here now—so I'm just trying to...

Stephen: If there's anything to do, we talked about this before—you can do what you are, but it's not a doing. It's a seeing, a noticing, because we are this consciousness. So we can say, noticing, period. If there's anything else other than the noticing or the seeing, the witnessing, the awareness—if there's anything else after that—if we think, oh, if I notice more, if I witness more, if I tune into the seeing more, then I'll get some result out of it, and I'll be free of the me sense—that's right back into the doing. As soon as that ego sense comes up, or the uncomfortable sense of resistance comes up, we think, oh, if I witness now I can get rid of this. Do you see that's right back into the doing and the suffering? I'm not being dogmatic.

Jason: No, that's the reality of it.

Stephen: Yes, that's trying to *do* the witnessing, or the watching, or the noticing—trying to *do* it is going right back into the problem. The problem is trying to do something—trying to resist the unpleasant, or grasp onto the pleasant. Now we're using this technique of witnessing to grasp onto the pleasant, and avoid the unpleasant. So we're right back into the suffering.

Jason: Right.

Stephen: There's nothing to do. But if we insist on doing something we can say, well, what I am is this witnessing. And just noticing, oh, I am the witnessing. But if there's any thought that if I can just witness more, then I'll be free, you're right back into the problem again.

Jason: The one word, *noticing*, really clears it up.

Stephen: Yes, just noticing. What can happen is there's actually an appreciation of that sense of me, that ego sense. When the sense of being an individual comes up, it's noticed. There can be an appreciation of the ego sense, being a separate me, because you're not fighting it anymore. You recognize fighting is futile—fighting anything. Fighting the ego sense is futile. If we say, I'm going to witness the ego hoping it will go away, we're back into the struggling!

If there's anything to do—we watch, we witness, we observe, we see. And there can be an appreciation of this me sense, this ego— there's an appreciation of it and you get the sense that, you know what? I like being me, I like being a person, I like the play of relationship—I love it! You love when you succeed, you love when you fail—you wouldn't have it any other way.

You're witnessing it—I am the witnessing presence of it. You can be laughing one moment, and crying the next. Relationships are perfect, and the next day they're terrible, and there's a love of it. Even when you're really uncomfortable, your relationships are terrible, and the finances are not good, there's an appreciation of it all. You may wonder what if *everything* in my life really goes to hell, what will that be like?

This awareness that we are, this consciousness is the love that loves hate. This is the peace that's at peace with war. This is where all the opposites come together. What I am is the witnessing presence of it all. So this is unconditional love, what I am. It loves hate. It loves sadness. It's happy about sadness. It's at peace with war. It's what I am. You don't have to do anything to be it, you are it. And there never was a problem with the challenges in life, with the relationships, the career, the finances, all those difficulties. They're really not problematic.

Your real nature is the one perfect, free, and actionless consciousness, the all-pervading witness—unattached to anything, desireless and at peace.
—Ashtavakra Gita

19

I Realized there's No 'Me' to Get Enlightened

Jason: The whole purpose of my spiritual search was to enlighten 'me'. I finally realized there's no 'me' to be enlightened! It's quite a shock to your system. After doing everything to make yourself better, you find there's no one here, and it's a shock to your system. It's kind of a shock.

I was reading a passage by Robert Powell, who edited some of Nisargadatta's books, and he talks about how the first taste of this is very bitter, but it turns to sweetness. And that's right. There are no ifs, ands, or buts about it—it's the cleanest, clearest. I don't know how you could get any clearer. I found out there's not a Jason here to be enlightened. It's not another addition, or a merit of honor of some sort.

Sean: I find that difficult, too. Because the bigger your ego the more difficult it is to get rid of it. It's as if we like the drama—is that what it is? We're addicted to the drama? We're addicted to who we think we are? Is it a process? Was your experience a process to get it, or did it just click or pop? I asked you that before.

Stephen: When I saw what John Wheeler was talking about, then everything else made sense—everything I'd ever read from the Bible, the New Testament, Christian Mysticism, Buddhism, Hinduism. They appear to be very different on the surface. But when you dig down to the essence of them, they seem to be the same.

Seeing the fundamentals clearly, everything else gets blown away. Nothing else matters anymore—the ego and enlightenment. Enlightenment is irrelevant. The ego is irrelevant. All of that gets blown away. And your left with the basics that, in my view, all of the ancient traditions point to. You'll see your questions are irrelevant, and you wonder, why did I even ask that question? It's completely irrelevant, it's meaningless!

We turn to different paths to get free of that heavy sense of ego—alcohol—you can get rid of the ego for a while with alcohol. But it comes back and you tend to do stupid things while you were drunk and make things worse. There are many ways to get rid of this me sense, the sense of being separate, and not good enough. We turn to alcohol, we turn to drugs, we turn to work, and attainment. If I can make more money, get a bigger house, more women, more cars, more respect. Then you fulfill those desires, but you still feel the sense of separateness, the sense of emptiness—attaining all those things leaves you empty still.

People turn to religion and spirituality thinking, well, this will do it! For a while you feel better, and then you hear of enlightenment! And you say, oh, this is it! I won't need any of that other stuff because I'll be enlightened! So we work and struggle for years to be enlightened. We see many teachers and gurus who we assume are enlightened. Everyone is bowing down to them, bringing gifts, and traveling from all over the world to see them. And we think, oh, that must be great!

Jason: Plus, they're perfect!

Stephen: Yes, they're perfect. They're never angry, they're always happy. They're always peaceful, loving and kind—and blissful.

Jason: They don't even go to the bathroom!

Stephen: No. So, of course we want to be enlightened! So we struggle for years and years to be an enlightened person. After a while you realize it's the same thing. It's me wanting to be special—I want to be *really* special. I want everyone to come see me and bow down to me because I'm so special—I'm enlightened! But striving for enlightenment there's still the egoic sense of wanting to attain something. But it seems spiritually correct because now we've thrown away the world, we're better than that! We're not interested in money, cars, houses, and worldly things. We're better than that—we're interested in spiritual things! We want to be the *spiritual* person, always loving, kind, and wise. And everyone comes to us for wisdom and love. That's the same egoic desire to be special.

You get to a certain point when you realize that's just more nonsense. And you're ready to give up. You get to the point when you're ready to hear the bottom line. You're ready to hear the truth. Alright, no more baloney, no more nonsense—I need to know the bottom line. That's when there's openness to the fundamentals—looking into what I am in essence, and what I am not.

I live; yet not I, but Christ lives in me. —**Galatians**

20

So, What's the Problem?

Stephen: So, what's the problem? Why do we have psychological suffering?

Sean: This is the part I was waiting for. It's the mind—or wanting to be somewhere other than where you are. Wanting to be somewhere else?

Stephen: The misconception of believing we're something we're not is at the root of suffering. That's when the appearance of suffering happens. And that's the other side of the coin—it's what I am *not*.

If I am simply this 'I am'—this consciousness, how does psychological suffering happen?

If we're clear on how suffering happens, when it comes up in your life—tomorrow, the next day, next week or next month—you've seen it clearly so it won't sneak up on you anymore. It can come in and you'll say, oh, I know what you are!

What's happening when there's psychological suffering? In your own experience, what's happening? The first thing you notice is that thoughts, stories, and images are happening, right? If there are no thoughts happening, no story and images happening, there's no psychological suffering.

When you're sitting and watching the baseball game, you're not thinking, and there's no suffering. If you're a musician and you're playing an instrument, or you're involved in doing your work, or you're driving—whatever you're involved in, there's no suffering. So the first thing we notice about psychological suffering is that it's when *thinking* is happening. Thinking is happening, images and stories are playing—that's the first thing we notice.

The second thing we notice about psychological suffering is that the thoughts, stories and images all revolve around whom? *Me!* If you're not thinking about 'me', and there's no image of Sean in your head, there's no suffering. You have an image of Sean, and Jason you have your image, and I have an image of Stephen—an image. We all have images of who we think we are. At the root of psychological suffering is the belief that this image of Sean or Jason is who you are.

If there are negative thoughts, disturbing feelings or sensations, and your experience is uncomfortable then Jason must be doing something wrong! Jason is not good enough! Something is wrong with Jason.

Jason: And the focus goes on trying to manipulate the image rather than checking if the image is real or not.

Stephen: Yes, there's the self-image and the assumption is this image—which is just an image—can exercise control and have only positive thoughts, only positive experiences. The belief is it can attain control—somehow. Through meditation, reading books, going to see teachers, getting enlightened—somehow it's got to take control.

So we say, okay, I'm going to make this practical. I'm going to take control of my thoughts—right now. See if you can do it. See if you can control your next thought.

Sean: I can. I can.

Stephen: What's your next thought going to be? Cell phone! [holding up a cell phone]

Sean: When you just said that...

Stephen: Your thought is now 'cell phone' and you had no idea it was going to be 'cell phone.' And now it's 'bottle'. [holding up a bottle] There's no way to know!

Sean: Well, the thought I was thinking came in, and I controlled it.

Stephen: Okay.

Sean: I'm not playing devil's advocate or contrarian because I really embrace Advaita and it feels good. But by nature I am very inquisitive. When you said to take control of your next thought, the thought of a beautiful woman came into my mind. I was able to control that.

Stephen: [laughing] Why didn't a picture of...

Sean: Mona Lisa or some other image?

Stephen: Yes.

91

Sean: Because you asked me to control it, and I controlled it.

Stephen: Notice in your own experience any time there is psychological suffering happening, there's thinking, there are images, and there's a story. At the center of the story is Sean—the image of Sean. The assumption is this image can control its experience. Isn't that the assumption? Otherwise everything is just happening and there's a natural acceptance—everything is as it is. There's no fighting with your experience.

At the root of your suffering is your self image, and the assumption that this image, Sean, has control over thoughts feelings, sensations and actions.

Sean: I understand because in my experience, my psychological suffering is obsessive. For example, with relationships I'll think, where did I go wrong? What did I do? Why did this happen? That's my experience. My thoughts are more obsessive about relationships. But, you're right, I'm not in control—the thoughts keep coming in, and keep coming in, and keep coming in. That's my psychological suffering. That's where my big issue is. Does it work the same way with other issues?

Stephen: Yes. The issue with relationships is there's this me image, this ego, and there's a natural sense of emptiness with this ego, and it can never be filled. The assumption in relationships is that someone else can fill the sense of emptiness and loneliness. So we turn to relationships, or to alcohol—pick your poison.

The egoic experience is one of separation, emptiness, loneliness, and it's always looking to be fulfilled. One way is through relationships. It's through this 'other' I can be fulfilled, this me image will be perfected. If she tells me I'm good, I'm a good guy—all of that—then this me image will get stronger and better.

When we see the self-image is just an image, we realize there's no 'me' here. There's no separate entity, no separate person. The image is seen to be just an image, it's not real. It can never be fulfilled. It can't be fulfilled through relationship. It can't be fulfilled with alcohol. It can't be fulfilled with money. It can never be fulfilled because it's just an image! There can only be a temporary sense of fulfillment. When the relationship is going well, and she's giving you positive feedback—you're a great guy, the self-image gets bigger and better.

Sean: My false sense of self.

Stephen: Yes, I am this image of Sean, and I am a good guy. Then she says one negative word and the balloon bursts. The image is deflated. And depression happens, what did I do wrong? I need to improve. Next time I'll be better. Did I do something wrong? Maybe I chose the wrong woman? It all revolves around this me image.

What I'm pointing out is seeing that all suffering, whether it's triggered by relationship or anything else—at the root of suffering is this self-image.

All psychological suffering and spiritual seeking get resolved in seeing what I am, this consciousness. And seeing what I am not—I am *not* this self-image.

If I have no images at all about myself, then what is there to see? There is absolutely nothing to see, and one is frightened of that. That is: one is absolutely *nothing*. But we can't face that, therefore we have those images about ourselves. —**J. Krishnamurti**

Seeing What I Am Not

Stephen: It's critical to see what you *are* in essence. Noticing, oh, yes, this *seeing*, this consciousness, I know this. This can't be denied. Your whole life there's been this *seeing*. This consciousness has always been happening and it can't be denied. You don't have to be convinced. But what *can* be denied is that you are separate—a separate entity who has control over his experience.

Jason: Every time I come up here I get more. I'm the kind of person who has to hear it. I've read it, but when I hear it in person there's something about it, and I get it. I get a clarification each time, and I got a big clarification tonight.

I've been very much identified with my story. I've been focusing on what I am. Stephen has pointed that out so clearly, it's impossible to debate, you cannot deny it.

But I have not been looking at what I am *not*. Tonight I'm really seeing my problems have been because of this self image, which I don't remember creating, but it's there. When I suffer it's the self-image at the root of suffering because there's an identity with it, and it seems real. But what is seeing the image? Well, it's being seen.

Stephen: By consciousness.

Jason: Consciousness. The image is only an idea. It's a concept. It's a self-concept. I'm speaking from what I'm experiencing right now. I'm not going by what I read, and it's not a metaphysical thing—I'm hearing it and seeing it. It's clear. It's like when I first saw the 'seeing'. I'm seeing the self-image now.

I'm not saying I've got it or not, I'm saying my experience in this moment is so clear. It's so clear. The key was seeing through this self-image, because for some reason it was eluding me, or hiding. Now the self-image is being seen by consciousness clearly.

I only have a problem when my self-image comes up in terms of maintaining its survival, or keeping it boosted up by my career or whatever the mind is going to bring up—that's the only time I suffer. It's only when the 'I' starts coming in there are problems—that's when the self-image comes in.

Everything is Falling Into Place

Jason: This is my fifth or sixth time here. Things have evened out for me without any effort. All my emotional stuff has leveled out. The right decisions seem to be made. I seem to be doing the right thing at the right time. I'm not reacting to what I did two months ago. It's still happening, but I'm not involved with it, or I'm minimally involved.

Everything is getting less reactive. Everything is happening without effort. It's not, okay, I can't react to that. It's, oh, yeah, I know who I am, which Stephen pointed out without doubt, and it's here. It's experiential for me. Sometimes I think about it, sometimes I don't. Everything is falling into place nicely.

Lenny: How did that happen—to get to this point?

Jason: I've done a lot of different things, a lot of different modalities. Advaita always captured me—Ramana Maharshi and several others. But most of them you can't sit down with in this kind of format and talk about it. Most people are not available on the East coast [USA]. So when I saw Stephen's website, I thought here's someone I can go see.

I remember the first time I came up here Stephen immediately pointed out who I am. I experienced it myself as I always am—consciousness, awareness, presence or however you want to describe it. It's undeniable. It's what you are right now. It's what we all are. When you see it yourself, oh, yeah! It's here all the time, for me anyway.

The more you see who you *are*, and see what you are *not*, and then go back and forth between the two, it neutralizes and everything is happening on its own. There's been no effort on my part to make any changes. It's happening by itself. My old stuff is still there, but I'm paying less attention to it. It's not getting my attention. It's, oh, yeah, you again! Okay, next, next.

Lenny: What do you do when things are not going well or the right way?

Jason: I've had some bad days, and I just watch. I don't like it, but I just watch. So you watch. Nothing you can do about it.

Lenny: How do you avoid getting involved?

Jason: There can be a fire burning here. I'm going to stay as far away as possible. Or I can go stick my face in the fire again. Staying away from the fire I may get a few singed hairs, but I'm not sticking my head in it—which I've done everyday for forty years.

So, that's what's going on. I've seen this show before, and I'll probably see it again. I know what it is. It doesn't catch me. Same old stuff—nothing new. I haven't decided to be uninvolved; I'm just not involved as much. I don't know what's going to happen tomorrow or ten minutes from now, but I know this is what's been happening.

The traveler has reached the end of the journey! In the freedom of the Infinite he is free from all sorrows. The fetters that bound him are thrown away, and the burning fever of life is no more.
—**The Dhammapada**

23

How Do I Avoid Involvement with the Character?

Lenny: How can I be aware of, and avoid involvement and identification with the character?

Stephen: Let's notice what we *are*. Then we'll look into the character with which there seems to be an involvement. And we'll look into how involvement happens. Seeing it clearly once is enough. It's not something you have to do all the time, or continue doing. Once you see the mirage in the desert is not a lake, you know it's a mirage.

You're walking with a friend in the desert and you're thirsty. There appears to be a body of water ahead, and your friend says, no, that's a mirage. He suggests you look into it, just look, and if you squint your eyes you'll notice it's heat rising from the desert floor. It's not water. So you look, but you still see a lake.

You say, well, I still see a lake. He says, squint your eyes a bit and look again. So you do it. You look and you realize it's only heat vapors rising. Then your eyes go back to the normal view, and it appears to be a lake again. But you know it's not a lake because you've seen it. You only need to see it once, and you're cured of the misconception of seeing a lake. Even though it appears to be a lake, you know it's only a mirage.

The same is true of seeing through the character, Lenny. There is a character, Lenny, who has his relationships, career, finances—all of that. There's the person and a body there. We're not saying it doesn't exist. We're looking into and seeing what we are in *essence*. Lenny always changes, his story always changes. He's happy and then he's sad. He has joy one moment and anger the next—and all the human emotions.

Lenny is always changing. But the consciousness is always the same. It's noticing, witnessing or seeing the character Lenny and his relationships, emotions, feelings and experiences.

Consciousness is watching it all. It's easy to see—this is really simple. Lenny, the person, is a character or an object in the consciousness—in what you are. You are the consciousness, and Lenny is an object in you. You are the witnessing presence of Lenny.

The object, Lenny, is no different than this cell phone. Notice the cell phone. Look at it and notice the colors, the buttons, and lights. The first thing we notice is the object—*now* notice the *seeing*.

Let's notice another object. Notice the fan which is a different object. It's not the cell phone. We're looking at the fan, and we notice the *seeing*. There's a *seeing* happening. The seeing of the fan—there's consciousness of the fan. The objects are different, but the seeing, or the consciousness is the same. We can notice any object, and then notice the seeing—there's a seeing.

There's a character called, Lenny. There's a body and it has relationships, a career, finances, all of that—pleasure and pain, happiness, sadness, and all the emotions. Lenny is always changing. His life situation is always changing. But the seeing, the consciousness is always the same. You are the consciousness watching Lenny and his story. It's the same as seeing the cell phone. You see Lenny as an object. This remote control is an object in consciousness, just like Lenny. Everything is an object in consciousness—in you.

I am the consciousness. Everywhere I go the consciousness is the same. The objects of consciousness are changing. Sitting here we see the chairs and we see all the objects in the room, there is consciousness. The objects are different, but the consciousness is the same.

Everywhere you go this consciousness is with you—you are it. Everywhere you go consciousness is here.

You have no identification with simple objects—there's no emotional involvement. There's a cell phone, there's a remote control—no problem. Because you don't believe you are this remote control. Lenny doesn't believe he is the remote control. You know you are *not* this remote control. It's an object in you. If you believe you are this remote control, you'd be identified and involved.

See that you are *not* the object, Lenny—Lenny is a character in consciousness. Lenny is a character in you! You are consciousness, and Lenny is in you.

You are pure Consciousness, the witness of all experiences. Your real nature is joy. Cease this very moment to identify yourself with the ego.
—**Shankara**

24

The Universe Says, 'Meow!'

Stephen: There's no one here. There's no Lenny who is in control. It's just an image, a story, thoughts, feelings, sensations, memories—all of that.

So how does that change your life experience? Seeing there's no separate, controlling entity here, the resistance to whatever is happening falls away. There are no more 'I should or I shouldn't' thoughts. There's no 'I'. And there's no assumption that 'I' am in control of anything.

[A loud 'meow' is heard in the background.]

The cat meowed. There's no control there. It just cried, meow. If the cat had the thoughts, 'I shouldn't interrupt the meeting, I should be quiet. What's wrong with me? He told me not to interrupt the meeting. There I go again!' If the cat had those thoughts, 'I shouldn't interrupt the meeting; I shouldn't scratch myself in front of everyone, what's wrong with me?' Then the cat would have psychological suffering. But there's no psychological suffering with the cat. There's just, 'meow,' and he walks into the other room—it's over. He's not in the other room thinking, 'what a bad cat I am, I can't believe I did that, I've been meditating for so long.' He's been attending all the meetings; he should get this by now! There's no sense of 'me' there.

Do you see how at the root of psychological suffering is the belief in the existence of a separate character, Lenny, Jason, or Stephen? There's a belief in the central character, the image, and the belief is this image, this me has control. And this image is able to exercise control over thoughts, feelings, sensations, actions—one's life experience.

There's a belief that somehow Lenny was able to separate himself from the rest of the universe, and then exercise control over the universe. The universe is expressing itself, not Lenny. Lenny is not expressing himself—there's no Lenny. Lenny is an expression of the universe.

All of your thoughts, all of your feelings, all of your actions are not yours. They're an expression of the universe. Whatever is expressing through this body is not Lenny's expression.

When the cat cried, 'meow,' that's not the cat expressing himself. That's the universe expressing itself through the cat. There's no separate, controlling entity there, and there was never a belief in one. There was never the belief, 'I am Ben the cat, and I am in control!'

Whatever's happening is an expression of the universe, an expression of the One—the One Essence. So everything in the universe is an expression of the Mysterious Source of all existence. Every thought that arises in your experience, every feeling, every sensation, every action—EVERYTHING is an expression of the One—the One Mysterious Source of all existence.

If anger arises here, did Lenny create the anger or did the Mysterious Source create the anger? If loving kindness is expressed through Lenny, is Lenny expressing the loving kindness? Is Lenny able to separate himself from the Source of the universe, and exercise control over thoughts, feelings, sensations, and actions—is that possible? So everything that's arising is an expression of the One Mysterious Source. So we see in our own experience this is what is meant by the pointer, 'All is One.'

See now the whole universe with all things that move and move not, and whatever thy soul may yearn to see—See it all as One in me.
—Bhagavad Gita

My Seeking for Enlightenment has Come to an End

Jason: My spiritual seeking has just, bang, stopped. I still love to read, but it's just for my own entertainment. When reading sometimes I see that's such a nice way of looking at it—beautiful. Seeing different perspectives is like listening to different musicians—it's just beautiful. But I'm not looking for a teacher or an experience. I always thought it was a metaphysical experience. I thought some light was going to come in and a chakra was going to open. Those things may happen, but those things are seen as happening in consciousness. People chase after mystical experiences for years and years. But it doesn't last, it goes. And you're back where you started—sometimes worse. Because then you're trying to chase after another experience.

When I was younger I had experiences that lasted for three or four months. I had absolutely ecstatic states of consciousness. I can't regain the state of consciousness that was going on! I have no idea what it was, and I'm not going after it any more.

I'm not searching for anything now. I know who I am. I know I'm consciousness. And I know what I'm *not*.

Sometimes I get lost in the story, not really, but that's part of the story, too, being lost in the story. I find the more I hear this when I come up here, the less the story is grabbing me. Maybe it's coincidence, but my life seems to be going better for me. I'm not reacting and obsessing over the same thoughts. Those thoughts come, and it's okay. They don't go after me anymore—or less and less.

I'm not thinking about the future as much. I'm not thinking about the past as much. It's just here I am. Nothing has changed, but in a certain sense everything has changed. There's no blast of light coming out of my head. And there's no concept to become enlightened.

When I started doing this it was, okay, I have to get this separate entity enlightened. I have to have spiritual experiences, a kundalini awakening. Because I thought that was the way. But that's just another experience happening in consciousness! So you think that's it, but that's not it! It's another story. If some guru has all those things happen, maybe he thinks that's who he is. Oh, I have power! I can do shaktipat! But that's just another story going on. And that story is going to come to an end. Just like my story.

Who Gets Enlightened?

Stephen: If there's any awakening, there's an awakening to the story that's happening. There's no person who awakens. The person is an image. Consciousness is already awake. Consciousness is awake-ness. Consciousness was never asleep.

But what happens in the human experience is the sense of being a separate person develops. From the time we're about two years old it starts developing and gets bigger and bigger. You can see it in your own experience. So the concept develops of 'me', the me image, and the story. It's a dream, it's a story.

There is no psychological suffering unless a dream story is playing. So there can be an awakening to the dream. In other words, you see this me image is only a story. So I'm awakened to the dream, or there's an awakening to the dream. But the dream character, Sean, didn't wake up. He was seen to be a dream character. So there's an awakening to the dream. I like how Leo Hartong puts it. There's no person who awakens. Sean doesn't become an enlightened person.

Jason: The self-image—that's what I was talking about. Trying to enlighten the mental image of yourself is the same as trying to make a million dollars or trying to gain fame.

Stephen: Right, we were talking about that earlier. Enlightenment is just the spiritually correct way or approach to attain the ultimate.

We are only dreaming. We dream that we are awake, we dream we are asleep.
Treating everything as a dream liberates. As long as you give reality to dreams, you are their slave. By imagining that you are born as so-and-so, you become a slave of so-and-so. The essence of slavery is to imagine yourself to be a process, to have a past and future, to have a history. In fact, we have no history, we are not a process. We do not develop, nor decay—so see all as a dream and stay out of it.
—Nisargadatta Maharaj

The Garden of Eden

Stephen: How do I know if I'm loving and kind? How do I know what love is? I don't know! I know nothing! I know nothing prior to eating from the tree of the knowledge of good and evil—prior to exercising the intellect, the mind.

There's no way to know what the enlightened state is unless we filter it through the mind. The mind is the known or believed to be true. What if we know that the only thing we know is we know *nothing*? The mind is just a bunch of concepts, ideas and beliefs that were force fed to us from the time we were children and through our adult lives. The mind is nothing but thoughts, memories, beliefs, assumptions, classifications, judgments—all of that.

Prior to the mind all there is, is this simple consciousness, this awareness that I am. And now we're living in the Garden of Eden. We don't know good from evil. Whatever thought happens in my experience, to me, this applies to me, to you, to you, to everyone— whatever happens in our experience there's no way to know if it's good or evil—if it's loving kindness or if it's selfishness. I don't know!

What is selfishness when there's no me and there's no you? Who is selfish to whom, for whom, for whose benefit? Who am I? I know *nothing* prior to eating from the tree of the mind—prior to eating from the tree of the knowledge of good and evil. There's no way to know what loving kindness is or what selfishness is. We can't say that one is right and one is wrong. We don't know what's right or wrong. Everything is just happening.

But of the tree of the knowledge of good and evil, thou shalt not eat: for in the day thou eatest therof thou shalt surely die.
—Genesis

Playing in the World of Duality

Stephen: There can be a sense of being a separate person, and that's part of the play. In these different bodies there's a sense of being a separate me, and now we can play.

Apparently the universe wants to enjoy itself. So the appearance of separation happens, and now we can be friends or we can be enemies. There's the play of relationship. There's the appearance of separation as if there are separate entities here. So the sense of being separate doesn't have to go—it comes and goes on its own. But when it comes up, it's clearly seen to be false, it's seen to be part of the play. So we play along. There's a sense of being friends or enemies. But there's the underlying sense that I know there's no separation, and I'm just going along with the play. There can be attachments. I am attached to the Red Sox. They're my favorite team. But I know there's no difference in essence between the Red Sox and the Yankees—in essence. But imagine how bored you'd be if you were watching the Red Sox playing the Yankees and you were completely indifferent.

Jason: Then you wouldn't be watching baseball.

Stephen: You don't care.

Stanley: Well, that's the state I'm in. [laughter]

Jason: I always say, they don't follow my career, and I don't follow theirs.

Stephen: There can be an attachment to our own children—when we're watching them play sports or in their other endeavors. Of course we want ours to be better and beat the others in any sort of competition—whether it's in sports, scholastics, a spelling bee, or any competition. Of course we want ours to win! The assumption is that if enlightenment happens I'll see that all is one and I'll have no attachment to anything or anyone. I won't have any attachment to 'my' child; there won't be this idea of 'my' child. Yes there is! There's a realization that all is one, but I still want my child to beat your child because I enjoy the play of it all!

It's like being attached to the Red Sox. I want to feel what it's like to win, and I want to feel what it's like to lose. I want to be happy. I want to be sad. I want to be dejected when they lose; I want to be elated when they win. The same is true with our children. The assumption is, well, if I see that all is one I shouldn't have any attachment to my child—why not? It's my child. I want my child to win! I want the elation when my child wins, and I want to be dejected when my child loses.

But you know it's not 'my' child and there's no difference between me and you. But that's boring. That's complete apathy and indifference. We want to be attached. So we watch and we enjoy the play of life. We love being attached. And we love being *de*tached sometimes. So it's all part of the play, and we wouldn't have it any other way. We want to win, and we want to lose. We want to be happy, we want to be sad. We want to laugh, we want to cry. We want it all.

There's no right or wrong. There's no constant state of bliss or constant state of anything. There's no constant state of union, no constant state of oneness. It comes and goes and we play in it. There's an underlying sense that all is one and the play doesn't matter. But even then the play of relationship happens—the sense that I'm separate from you, and maybe we're boxers fighting. Or we're friends going to the baseball game together

We love all of it. It's all free to come and go. None of it is right or wrong. There's no such thing as right or wrong. There's no enlightened state. There's no constant state of union.

There is an underlying sense that all is one, but we go into the play of relationship. You can sit and meditate and there's nothing. Or when you're driving at times there's nothing, just absolute peace and relaxation. Then we've had enough of that. Now I want to be back in the play again. I want to be back in the play of relationship. I want the possibility of success and I want the possibility of failure. I want the possibility of healthy relationships and I want the not so healthy relationships. I want to feel it all.

You could hang out in the absolute sense of nothingness. It's not a sense of union it's a sense of the absence of division. That's why Advaita is a good way to put it, not two, rather than I am the one. There's not two, there never was two. There's the absence of division and we can hang out in that, so to speak. And after a while it gets boring. We want the division. We want the sense of two-ness.

29

I Wanted to be Superman as a Kid

Stanley: Well, when you're dealing with omnipotent, omniscient, and omnipresent consciousness, there's nothing, even the slightest little experience, or the slightest little thought that isn't just the 'I' experiencing. And, so, as Nisargadatta says, the 'I' is the same whether it appears to be an individual or not. He used some word, I think it was something like the infinite focused—*focused*, that's what he said—focused as an individual. It's focused. Sure, there's the sense of position in space within the dream here, but there's only one 'I'. And that's the only thing that hangs people up—the belief that there's more than one 'I'. But even the sense of there being separate I's, is the one 'I' expressing itself all at the same time. People don't grasp the absolute creational power that's involved in all the simultaneous multiple dream creations that are going on.

Stephen: All from the same Source.

Stanley: It's absolutely stunning.

Stephen: Nisargadatta talks about that in *I AM THAT*. Someone said to him, I'm sitting here and you're sitting there—we're not the same. He said there are different points of consciousness, but there's one awareness.

When the thought 'I', or 'my' arises, and my consciousness is separate from your consciousness—as soon as that thought arises, the appearance of separation happens. But it's only an appearance! It's an image of me over here with my own power and consciousness, and you over there. It's an image. It's a story playing. When that story is not there, there is no I, no me, and there's no you. There's no right, there's no wrong. There's no up, there's no down. There's nothing prior to thought.

Prior to the thought and image of 'I, me, mine' there is no separation—there's just consciousness. This is not a special state. You can notice when the I thought arises throughout your day. You may notice the absence of the I thought when you're focusing on whatever you're doing—fixing your car, making breakfast, working on your computer. Then the I thought arises, 'I have to do this or that.' The I thought is usually relative to some other person, some other expectation—I, I, I. That is the birth of the appearance of separation.

Jason: I take the subway quite frequently and I see a lot of people. I see all as consciousness, but I see everybody is in their story. Everybody's got a story, just like my story. Oh, how many stories? It's unbelievable! But without the stories it's all one—it's all one. We all experience our stories, our stories can be fantastic. There's more and more— chapter one, chapter two. It goes on and on. It never stops, it's infinite.

Stephen: Seeing that the story is just a story, there's quite a relief. Prior to seeing the story as a story, the story was believed to be true. The central character in the story, of course, is *me*. Everything revolves around me. Seeing the whole drama is not true, it's just concepts and images, the story can continue. It doesn't matter if there's a story playing. It's just another object in consciousness and you can see all the different stories. You see it's a nonsense story, and then you watch all the stories come and go.

Jason: In the past couple of months I've really been hands-off with my life situation. I've been just watching what's happening. Everything is clearing out by itself. I'm not thinking I shouldn't be worrying about this or that, it's just happening all by itself without me getting involved. I don't know why.

Stephen: It's a much more pleasant way to live. It's much easier to live that way. Everything is just happening.

Jason: My stress level has gone down so much. My life situation hasn't changed substantially at all.

Stephen: There's a new perspective on it.

Jason: Yes, I'm not worrying about money. I'm not worrying about the future. I'm just doing what I'm doing. The 'I should' thoughts are gone—I should be doing this, I shouldn't have done that—no! This is it. And you know something? I'm enjoying it. I'm kind of enjoying it.

Stephen: That's why I share this message. There is a benefit to folks who see this. I know there was for me. I figure if this can help me, and

107

it's so simple, it can help others. I feel I have to share this. It's so simple, and I struggled for so long with this. It's too simple for a lot of people—they want to be in the story of enlightenment.

Jason: That's a good story, too.

Stanley: That can be inspiring.

Stephen: It's another story.

Jason: I wanted to be Superman when I was a kid. Everybody wanted to be Superman, or Roy Rogers or whatever. That's fine.

Here a star, and there a star
Some lose their way
Here a mist, and there a mist
Afterwards—day!
—Emily Dickinson

30

No Suffering—No Enlightenment—No Embodiment

Stephen: If people think they're going to get enlightened, then there's a story playing. I felt that, too.

Jason: Yeah, we all do.

Stephen: There's an image of a person suffering. I didn't think it was an image, I thought I was actually suffering. But it's a story. As soon as you see you were never suffering—for twenty years I thought I was suffering. I wasn't suffering, it was a story playing creating a disturbance in the body, and there's a belief that the story is true. And the character at the center of the story is suffering, and the character can do something to attain enlightenment. So then he'll be an enlightened person.

But when you see there's only consciousness, the whole story falls apart. There's no one to get enlightened, and there was never anyone suffering. It was happening in the story, as a story. That's why you'll hear people say, there's no enlightenment. At the same time, you see there was never anyone suffering. It all gets thrown away. All there is, is consciousness and the stories that are playing—stories of a suffering person and stories of an enlightened person. They're all stories and they're not true. The only thing that's true is I am, this consciousness is, and you're done. There's nothing else. There are no levels of attainment. There's nothing.

Whatever happens after that is an appearance in the story. This idea of embodying the awakening is another story appearing in consciousness. But I'm not going to suffer over that idea, trying to embody the enlightenment—I'm done with that. That *is* the suffering—trying to embody, trying to attain, trying to be loving, kind and peaceful, trying to be enlightened. That *trying* is the very suffering I wanted to be free of! I'm not interested in embodying anything! Whatever's happening is happening. I watch.

There may be a change in behavior, I don't know. But I'm not going to measure it. I'm not interested in that. Whatever behavior happens—there may be more loving kindness happening, I don't know! It's not me doing it, and I don't want any part of it. Because as soon as you say, I'm going to embody this awakening, I need to be loving, kind and peaceful all the time, I need to emanate this loving, kind, peaceful energy, then I'm right back into the story, right back into the suffering—which is the very suffering I'm trying to be free of!

That's why I throw away all ideas of embodiment and any sort of expectation of how the behavior should change after it's realized there's no one here creating the behavior! There's just consciousness. If anyone gets that, the whole concept will be burned out—there's no one to get enlightened. There's no enlightenment, and there's no one who's *un*-enlightened. It's just a story, a concept—it does exist as a concept. There is a concept of enlightenment. But it's only a concept!

Jason: We could ask, does the mind become enlightened? Does the body become enlightened? Is there such a thing as enlightenment?

Stephen: Anyone who is caught up in the concepts of enlightenment will have all sorts of expectations—well, you should be loving and kind, and emanate this positive, loving and kind energy—no! Kill the Buddha! If you see the Buddha on the road—if you see the loving and kind, peaceful Buddha on the road, kill him! [laughter]

If there are any concepts of how there should be loving and kind behavior all the time, kill it. This is what Huang Po is saying, there is no difference between all the Buddhas and all the sentient beings—they're all One Mind. So if there are any ideas that you should be loving and kind, or emanate any positive energy—kill it. [laughter]

I like some of the old Zen masters. They're really direct. It's so refreshing and clear.

There are no Enlightened men or ignorant men, and there is no oblivion. Even Enlightenment, the Absolute, Reality, Sudden Attainment—every one of them—are concepts; they have nothing to do with the Buddha-Mind.
—**Zen Master Huang Po**

110

31

This Ain't It-That Ain't It—Neti-Neti

Stephen: There are so many people who are seeking spiritually and suffering.

Gary: Everybody.

Eileen: Yeah.

Gary: Virtually everybody. I work in California about once a month, and everybody is seeking. In the Bay area particularly, down in L.A., too—Chicago, Santa Fe.

Stephen: When I saw this I was struck first by Nisargadatta's directness, and then by 'Sailor' Bob Adamson, and he suggested I talk to John Wheeler. So I flew out and met John, and he kept pointing out the fundamentals of this—what you are and what you're not.

Eileen: And that did it? Was there a defining moment or was it gradual?

Stephen: Well, reading all sorts of spiritual literature over the years, you almost can't help but have what you'd call experiences (at the time)—experiences of 'no me' while driving, working, or in your daily life.

Gary: In your daily life, yeah.

Stephen: You can't help but have those experiences (or what you think of as experiences at the time)—oh, that was an experience! Well, it turns out that's your natural state, this simple awareness that you are. Then we go back into the mind and think, I'm back to reality, the mind and thinking.

Gary: Right, I have to pay the rent...

Eileen: Blah, blah, blah, blah, blah.

Stephen: And we think that's reality (the mind stuff). We have things backwards. We think of the awareness, the consciousness, the underlying essence of what we are as an experience when we notice the simple presence of awareness that's very peaceful and at ease. We have experiences that seem to be triggered by reading or meditating— it happened with me over the years when everything would drop away and it was very peaceful.

Eileen: Yes.

Stephen: It would last for a few hours or a few days.

Eileen: And then...

Stephen: Then thoughts would come back in, and I'd think, okay, I'm back to reality. No, you're back to the dream!

Eileen: You're back to the dream.

Stephen: Yes.

Eileen: But when you're not in the dream, there's nothing you have to do.

Stephen: And no one to do it.

Eileen: And no one to do it.

Gary: Better yet!

Eileen: I had an experience for a whole day when my thoughts stopped completely, abstract thoughts stopped completely. I didn't do this, but in retrospect, it was huge. It was not at all the way I am now or the very next day. The little voices came back. That experience happened and it seemed to go away. It's even worse going through life like this because...

Stephen: You've had a taste, so to speak.

Eileen: Yes, I've had other tastes, but that was really—it got quiet, like the electricity went off, really quiet. This brain actually makes a lot of

112

noise. That was fifteen years ago, and it hasn't happened again. Okay, it's not really a happening, but there's no way to be okay after that experience.

Stephen: You had an appetizer, you're still hungry.

Eileen: You're still hungry and the suffering is back. I know Tony Parsons, and Gangaji talk about how everything is still there. The anger is still there, and all that kind of stuff. But during that day there were no abstract thoughts and there was no possibility of anger. There was no possibility of greed. None of these things could happen because they are a product of thought. The thought wasn't there, so the other stuff wasn't there. There was nothing to do, and there was nothing I saw that was wrong in the world.

Yet, accidentally on that day I found I actually had quite a lot of power. When I had a thought, a logistical thought, it was magic—things happened. But it wasn't intriguing to me because nothing was intriguing to me. It was not a dualistic state—like, wow, I can do stuff! I've not been able to get back to that place—and I know it's not really a place.

But what you were saying about yourself is kind of a reflection of what John Wheeler says in his book, then he went to see Bob Adamson.

Stephen: I can talk about when the seeking and psychological suffering were seen clearly. There was a point in time it was seen—okay, this is it, I don't have to seek and suffer anymore. But that almost gives it too much importance, making it seem like an event. It's a knowing that I'm done with the seeking. I am this simple witnessing presence, and everything is free to come and go. There's no one here creating the thoughts or feelings, they're just happening.

Gary: They arise, yes.

Stephen: There's no one here to do anything about them. For me the suffering was, as it is for you, Eileen, trying to get those pleasant experiences back. The suffering was in trying to get back to the state of the absence of thought. The state where everything was simple and peaceful, and there wasn't the possibility of disturbing emotions. It's this sense of not knowing. It's this absolute clueless-ness, and everything is just fine.

113

Eileen: Yes.

Stephen: Whether someone is yelling at you or hugging you, everything is beautiful, everything is fine. When we have those experiences there can be a natural desire to want to re-create them.

Eileen: Oh, yeah!

Stephen: That in itself...

Eileen: ...is the suffering.

Stephen: It *is* the suffering.

Gary: Or the block, the impediment.

Stephen: We're trying to re-create something that was very pleasant.

Gary: That you already are.

Stephen: Yes. These experiences you're talking about may not happen ever again. It may not happen ever again. And it doesn't have to happen again to live in peace. It may or it may not. There's no way to know what experiences will happen.

I remember an insight when I was fourteen, prior to reading any of this. I had not been introduced to any concepts, even psychological terms like the ego, never mind any sort of spiritual terms. At fourteen years old there was this sense that everyone I was with, when we say 'I', it's the same 'I'. It just struck me and I said it to everyone. I was at a friend's house and he said, "I am going to watch TV." His mother, who cooked dinner for us, said, "I am going to wash dishes." His sister said, "I am going to do homework." And I said, "I am going home." It just struck me and I said to them, "We're all the same 'I'." While walking home I realized when we say 'I' it's referring back to the same I, it's the same sense of I. When you feel the sense of I, it's the same sense I feel—it's this sense of being. Our stories are different, and we have different points of consciousness here in this room, but we're all the same in essence.

These experiences happen through the years and they keep us searching because we know there's more to life than getting a great job, making money and all of that—there's more to it. There's this

114

simple presence that we are, and this is the peace we're searching for, it's what I want. It's what I get, seemingly, when I accomplish things—when I make a lot of money, when my relationships are perfect, or when I'm given respect. When we get what we want, there's a sense of relief, there's a sense of peace. It turns out this peace has always been here. It just appears to be disturbed by trying to attain these other things.

Gary: Trying to make our life work out.

Stephen: Yes, trying to make our life situation work out. So we notice it's always here—this peace we want. We see it experientially over time. We have experiences through the years, and we try to get them back.

Gary: But what you're trying to get back, you already are that anyway.

Stephen: Yes, the spiritual seeking is the same as seeking for money, or seeking for respect, or for the best relationships—it's all the same. We're seeking after some *thing* to give us the sense of peace we want. When we see that, we throw away the spiritual seeking.

There are two key pointers I talk about and they apply to all of us. The ancient spiritual traditions point to this; that is looking into what you are by answering the fundamental question, who am I? Ramana suggested that and many others—Who am I? What am I?

Other traditions talk about the fact that the reason we suffer is due to the sense of being separate. And the resolution to suffering is through recognizing that all is one, and we're not separate from God, we're not separate from Universal Life, or Universal Intelligence— seeing there is no separate entity here.

My seeking and searching came to an end by looking into the fundamentals. John Wheeler suggested I look into what I *am* and what I am *not*. And answer those questions in my own direct experience. Not just conceptually saying, I am consciousness, I am one with God—we can answer them conceptually, but that's not enough. But answering and noticing in our own direct experience. He suggested I look into this me that I thought I was, who is Stephen?

I talked to him and said, "I'm suffering." I told my story, put everything out on the table—here's my story, I'm suffering. He said if you look in your own direct experience and see—'who' is suffering? Is there anyone there? Is there any separate entity called Stephen?

115

Is there any separate entity called Eileen or Gary? Can you find Eileen? Who is Eileen? Who is Gary? Looking in your own experience, is there any separate entity there at all?

Gary: Who is separate?

Eileen: So there's nobody there. You look and you can't find anything.

Gary: What's there is a story you made up.

Eileen: You look and you can't find anything. If you look further you find this alive nothingness. It's always been here. There's no definition to it. But is that enough? Is sensing that enough? Doesn't there have to be some sort of a flip?

Stephen: You see, that keeps us on the path!

Eileen: I'm on the path!

Stephen: I saw the same thing over the years. I know all there is, is consciousness, there's no one here, *but*—and then the yeah, buts! Yeah, but, what about experiencing universal love and union? Yeah, but, shouldn't there be loving kindness expressed all the time here? Shouldn't there be an absence of anger and negative thoughts? Shouldn't there be loving kindness, peace and thoughtful behavior all the time?

Gary: So you have a fixed image of what it should look like.

Stephen: Right. We have a fixed definition of what life should look like. We have experiences of the absence of 'me' and there's only consciousness, and we think, oh, this is it! It lasts a few hours, a few days, a few weeks, and then something or someone comes along and sort of pokes us, or stirs up the me image or ego sense. The ego sense comes back into play.

Eileen: You react.

Stephen: Maybe we yell or anger arises. Oh, I'm not supposed to have anger! I didn't have anger for several days, several weeks. Anger came up, what happened? What's wrong with me? I have to get it back. I did something wrong. Okay, what did I do to get it? Was I meditating?

Gary: Rather than seeing anger is part of it.

Stephen: Yes.

Gary: Being pissed off is part of it.

Stephen: If you look in your own direct experience for this me, this ego, the sense of being a separate, controlling entity who can exercise its own separate control—do you find one? So I'm looking for that entity, and this one is called Stephen. I'm looking and asking who is Stephen? Who do I feel I am in my gut? I'm doing this inquiry to find out who I am. What am I looking for? You can feel it in your chest and your stomach, this sense of resistance—I want this, I don't want that, it's a disturbing energy.

Eileen: It's a sensation, right?

Stephen: You can feel the sense of ego as an energy of resistance in your stomach or chest. When the sense of ego is absent, the energy of resistance is gone. What is this disturbing energy here? What is this? It's a sense of being in control. It's a sense that I am a separate, controlling entity—this ego. That's who Stephen is.

When this inquiry becomes your own personal inquiry, not something you read in a book—okay, Ramana said to ask who am I? Who am I? Who am I? Who am I? That's just conceptual, it's not really effective. When you define yourself as you believe yourself to be, who is this Gary character? Who is it? What do I feel I am? Who is Eileen? When you say, Eileen, what does that mean? What is this ego? What I noticed is it's the sense of being in control. It's a sense based on a belief that there is some sort of a controlling entity here. Because if anger arose, then a thought would follow, oh, I shouldn't be angry; I should be loving and kind. What does that imply? What does the thought, 'I shouldn't be angry,' imply?

Gary: There's a *you*.

Stephen: There's a me who can exercise control, and a me who created the anger.

117

Gary: You made the good stuff, and you made the bad stuff.

Stephen: Right, that's what it implies. Any 'I should' thought—I should always be loving, kind and peaceful; I should never be angry; I should always be selfless; I should never be selfish. You know, I should—fill in the blank.

Eileen: Always be happy.

Gary: Right, I should always be happy—thrilled! Not happy, thrilled!

Eileen: I should be ecstatic. I should be in a state of ecstasy.

Gary: And bliss.

Eileen: Bliss, bliss! I should be blissful. I should be in an ocean of bliss!

Gary: We saw Tony Parsons, and read his books. I got that whatever arises *is it*. And then I forgot about it, we moved across country again.

Eileen: That's something that could make you forget.

Gary: I started reading his books again and I think where I am now is I see stuff arise and if I'm not neutral about it, I get caught up in it. If I'm happy and I say, I'm happy and I love that, then I have a preference. The ego steps in and says, I like this, and I don't like that. So more and more I'm neutral about whatever arises.

We were driving today and had some bickering, and I reacted, but I also felt neutral about it. I didn't judge it or think it was terrible that I got pissed off. Anger arises. Happiness arises. But I'm not really doing any of it. For me I feel the least amount of suffering in my whole life, and I'm not really seeking.

Eileen: That sounds to me what Gangaji calls strategy. There are strategies you can employ to be more peaceful or neutral. You can catch yourself when you get caught up in thoughts. Tony Parsons said when you have feelings come up, and this is an enormously helpful strategy if you're into strategies, you can isolate the sensation. If you think about it, emotions are sensations that are attached to a thought. So if you let the thought go, and you can do this very easily because you can always get back to the thought—let the thought go, and concentrate on the sensation. The sensation begins to have its own color and flavor, and it actually changes.

But that's a strategy. You can go through life doing that kind of stuff and you can feel better and cope better. But it seems to me that is doing something. And if you're doing something, it's still dualism, you know?

Gary: Yes, but there's no *me*. It just arises. Things continuously arise and they can't even be stopped, as far as I can tell. You can't stop stuff from arising—it just arises. If I'm not neutral about what arises, then I'm locked into it and I'm dancing with the tiger.

Eileen: So that's all it is!? In which case it's sort of ass! Because anybody can do that, right?

Gary: No.

Stephen: Well, only 'special people' can do what you're talking about Eileen. You have to be special!

Eileen: [laughing]

Gary: Well, you say everybody can do it, it's everybody's nature, however, all the people I work with (I do body work, one-on-one) and I see a lot of people, and everybody has the 'I' down. When I say, "stuff arises," that's a whole new concept for people. They'll say, "I was pissed off," and I'll say, "well, being pissed off arose." And that's very different than "I'm pissed off."

Eileen: Yes.

Gary: It's different and there's no suffering in that.

Eileen: Right.

Gary: If I don't see it's just arising then I have suffering over it.

Stephen: There's no 'I' there doing anything. I'm going to continue talking about what you are and what you are not. This is what brought

119

the spiritual seeking and suffering to an end. It doesn't bring anger to an end or any other feeling.

Gary: Right—jealousy, fear.

Stephen: *Whatever* happens. It seems to me, Eileen, you have a definition of the behavior that should come out of this insight or recognition.

Eileen: Not behavior, but state of being.

Stephen: Is there an 'I' who has this state of being? Is there anyone there who *has* it?
　　Let's look into what you are in essence. There's one coin of what you are. There are two sides of that coin—what you *are*, and what you are *not*—seeing this in your own experience, not just conceptually. We want to answer the question, who am I, or what am I? We want to look at this from a positive and a negative perspective—what I am, and what I am not. Seeing what I am is very simple and pleasant, it's this consciousness that I am, this simple presence of awareness. Something is looking out of these eyes right now, something is hearing these words. It's not Stephen that's looking out of these eyes.

Eileen: Right.

Stephen: This looking is happening. The hearing is happening. The senses are active.

Gary: Right, you're sitting there, and these people arose in your living room.

Stephen: Yes, these characters, and this body arose in my experience. I have no idea where they came from or where they're going. There's this consciousness here. The only thing I know with absolute certainty is this witnessing is happening; this witnessing presence, consciousness or awareness—there's awareness here.

Gary: I call it 'watching'.

Stephen: This watching, this witnessing—whatever word works for you.

Gary: That works for me, 'watching'.

Stephen: This seeing is happening, hearing is happening, sensing is happening. Eileen has nothing to do with it. It's just happening.

Eileen: I got that.

Stephen: All of the senses are happening. This awareness is what you are.

Eileen: But that's no biggie!

Stephen: It's not good enough! You want more!

Eileen: That's just, okay, I got that part. I mean, yeah.

Stephen: Okay, so we see that. That's what we are—this awareness. Now we look into what we are not. If we look to our own direct experience and ask what's happening when we're suffering? And I'd say that my interest in sharing this message is to share the fact that it's possible to be free of spiritual seeking and suffering. That's my interest in sharing this message. That's what happened for me.

Gary: That is my interest in being here, too.

Stephen: What's happening when psychological suffering is happening? The first thing we notice is thoughts are happening, a story is happening. Thoughts and stories are happening, and they revolve around 'me', 'I'—Eileen, Gary, or Stephen. There's something wrong with me, something is not quite right, I'm not good enough. I need to be more loving, kind and peaceful. I should never be angry—I, me. I should be...you know the story of Eileen.

Eileen: What you're saying is stuff keeps happening to you.

Stephen: Let's look into that. There's a completely different perspective—like Gary was saying. It's not happening to *me*. Everything is *happening*.

Eileen: It's just happening.

121

Stephen: Nothing is happening to 'me'. These thoughts are not happening to 'me'.

Gary: And the war.

Stephen: It's not happening to 'me'.

Gary: It's got nothing to do with me.

Stephen: Right.

Gary: It just arises.

Stephen: Even the mental war playing in the head. This is the peace that's at peace with war. This is the love that loves hate. This is absolute, it's unconditional. This is the happiness that's happy with sadness. This is what I am—this witnessing presence.

When does psychological suffering happen, and what's happening? We notice there's thinking, and thinking about 'me'! There's no psychological suffering if I'm thinking about you!—or my cat or my dog. Only if it's in relation to me!—me and my story. Suffering usually involves thinking about something I did, or didn't do. I should be doing this, or I shouldn't be doing that. This 'I', this 'me' is at the center of all psychological suffering—see if that's true for you.

In your own direct experience see if every time psychological suffering is happening, thinking is happening, a story is playing, and Eileen is the central character in the story. She is the 'I' that should be doing this or that. She should be experiencing peace and love. She should be able to re-create blissful experiences—I, me, Eileen.

That's who I felt Stephen was—this energy of attachment and resistance. This is the ego, Stephen. So we look and see every time suffering is happening, there's thinking, a story, and it revolves around me—I should or I shouldn't. What is this me that says, I should or I shouldn't? Who should be creating the blissful experiences? Who should be avoiding the anger? Who should always be happy? Who? Is there anyone there?

You look in your own experience and see there is no separate, controlling entity (that's the term that makes sense to me). This is who Stephen felt he was—a separate, controlling entity—an entity here who can exercise its own control. That is at the root of all of my

122

psychological suffering. I should always be happy. I should never be selfish...I, I, I.

Gary: I should share.

Stephen: I should be sharing, and kind. I should...I, I, I, I, I. So what is this 'I'? Who is this 'I'? Who is this Stephen character? Is there anyone here creating anything? Or is everything arising in awareness? Anger arises. Happiness arises. Loving kindness arises. There's no Stephen here doing any of it! There's no Eileen doing any of it. There's no Eileen trying to re-create the blissful experiences, it's just happening in this awareness that you are.

There's no way to re-create a blissful experience. If you have any expectation whatsoever about how your experience should be, then you'll continue to suffer because there's an I who believes it should be blissful, loving and kind. It should always be as it was during your blissful experiences, and 'I' need to create that experience.

So we see there is no one here who ever created anything at all, everything is just happening. Everything is arising in this awareness that I am—as Gary put it.

Gary: Yes, try to stop it from arising—it's impossible!

Stephen: We say, okay, I've looked for this I, this me that I think I am, this separate, controlling entity—I've looked for it and found nothing. Maybe I've overlooked it. Let me see if I can exercise control. I haven't found any separate, controlling entity here, but I still believe I can control my experience. I still believe I should be loving and kind, I should never be selfish. I can't find any separate, controlling entity here, but let me see if I can *exercise* control over my experience.

Surely if there is some sort of a controlling entity or mechanism here, I should be able to exercise it! Shouldn't I be able to exercise control if it exists? So I'm going to sit here and try to exercise control. I'm going to have only positive thoughts. I'm going to see if I can have only pleasant experiences and sensations. Let's see if I can control my experience. Go ahead, try it! This makes it practical.

We've looked at it from a conceptual approach, and I can't find any controlling entity. Now we make it practical—if there is a controlling entity here, surely I can exercise control over my experience. Go ahead, take control. Why are you waiting? What are you waiting for? If there is any separate, controlling entity here called Eileen, she would have taken control of her experience by now. There is no separate, controlling entity there. Everything is happening.

To answer the question, who am I? We look at what I am, and what I am *not*. What I am *not* is this Stephen character, this ego, this me, this sense of being in control. There is no separate, controlling entity. So I looked and I found nothing! And I tried to *exercise* control over my experience. I'm not able to do it.

If I am *not* this Stephen character who I felt I was, then what am I? I can feel the sense of ego in my chest—this resistance. It's trying to control my experience, trying to hold onto the pleasant experiences and avoid the unpleasant. This resistance *is* the ego. The egoic experience is one of resistance and it can be felt here in the chest and stomach.

Eileen: Yes, exactly.

Stephen: I'm looking for a separate, controlling entity, and trying to exercise control—I can't do it. So it's seen that this Stephen character I thought I was, this ego, who has its own separate will and can exercise its will to create its own state of mind, its own thoughts, its own feelings, sensations, actions, and experiences—all of that. There's nothing here! There's nothing here.

What I find is an image of Stephen—stories, memories, a family, relationships, finances, career—all of that is a story. And when I look for a controlling entity, there's nothing! So I am not this Stephen character I thought I was. I am not a separate, controlling entity. It was a belief, a story, thoughts, images, and an energy of resistance, an uncomfortable energy. That's all I can find. I can find nothing with any control. So there is no separate, controlling entity here. I thought that was who I was.

Gary: As you were supposed to, as we were trained.

Stephen: As we were trained from the time we were little kids. As children no one ever pointed this out to us, at least not clearly.

Gary: Well, hardly anyone knows.

Eileen: It's in the culture. Lose weight; take control of your life! It's in commercials. Everything is about taking control. Oh, I feel I'm in control of my life!

Stephen: Yes, 'I' am in control. There is control but it's not a separate I. There is something controlling and moving all of this, but it's the same essence.

Gary: For everybody.

Eileen: It's what you already are.

Stephen: Whatever it is that makes the sun shine...

Eileen: Right.

Gary: Makes the bugs crawl.

Eileen: And your skin crawl!

[laughter]

Stephen: Whatever it is that makes the bugs crawl...

Gary: Makes the trees grow, the grass grow, the rain fall, everything.

Stephen: It's the same source that creates every thought, feeling, and sensation in your experience. Eileen does *nothing*. I call it the Mysterious Source of all existence. We can call it God, Universal Intelligence.

Gary: Or Larry.

Stephen: Or Larry—whatever you want to call it. It's a mystery.

Eileen: I like that—the Mysterious Source of all existence.

Stephen: It's a mystery. What makes a cat meow? What makes an oak tree grow leaves and acorns in the spring? It's a mystery. And it's the same Mystery—now this applies to you—it's not just creating the oak tree, the leaves and acorns, it creates every thought you have Eileen, every thought! Every thought, every feeling, every sensation is created by the same Mysterious Source! It's not possible that Eileen has ever done anything.

Gary: Even having the experiences of bliss.

Stephen: She did nothing!

Gary: Even the blissful experiences arose.

Stephen: She did nothing.

Eileen: It just arose.

Gary: Then you had a preference, I want that, I like that, I love that.

Eileen: I want it forever.

Stephen: Even *that* is not Eileen's wanting! Even the ego is not yours. Even the ego is an expression of the One Mysterious Source—even the ego! There's nothing Eileen has done. Everything is a creation of the One Mysterious Source! It's not possible for Eileen, or Gary or Stephen, or a cat, dog or oak tree to separate itself from the Mysterious Source of all existence.

It's born into this world, this Eileen character, and then somehow she separates herself from the rest of creation and is able to exercise control over thoughts, feelings, and sensations. It's not possible! There is no possible way Eileen could separate herself from the Mysterious Source of all existence. Nothing that arises in your experience is Eileen's creation—whether it's beauty or ugliness, whether it's loving kindness or selfishness. It is the One Mysterious Source expressing itself through Eileen. There's no Eileen. There's just consciousness, and that's what I am. I am this witnessing presence, this watching.

Gary: I like that, that's beautiful—witnessing presence.

Stephen: This is what I am!

Gary: Witnessing presence.

Stephen: This witnessing presence. This witnessing is happening. Witnessing the thoughts, the feelings, the sensations, the actions, the relationships, the finances, the career—*everything* is witnessed, and that's what I am. I am this watching. So, anger arises, wow, look at that anger!

Gary: Isn't that interesting.

Stephen: And sadness arises, oh, sadness.

Gary: How interesting.

Stephen: Happiness arises, whoa!

Gary: How interesting.

Stephen: How interesting. I'm not doing anything. There's no one here to do anything!

Gary: That's happening more and more for me. In the work I do I'm seeing more and more that everything is arising. There's no doer. I am as surprised saying it as you may be hearing it, but there's no doer. And have you noticed how good business has arisen?

Eileen: Yes.

Gary: What's arisen is a very successful business. Whereas for thirty years I've been busting my ass and what arose was poverty. Really, poverty had arisen to the point where it was a big thrill for us to go to the grocery store and shop for food. So I find myself disappearing in a sort of way. It's hard to explain.

Eileen: Yeah, I get it, I get it.

Stephen: Gary is talking about what I'm talking about.

Eileen: There's an attachment [here with me] to an idea of transcendence that has to do with the sense of being a separate, controlling entity.

Gary: Yes, that's arising, and you can love that. You can love it like you love the bliss that arose, because you're neutral about it. If you're not neutral, you get caught up in it. You love this, and you don't like that—then you're back trying to control your experience.

Stephen: There was a time I felt I was seeing things clearly. I was feeling a sense of ease and peace with very little mental churning and

127

thinking. Then the peace would be disturbed by something—any odd thing. Anger would arise, or a memory from a previous relationship would trigger off a series of upsetting thoughts, or I'd want a glass of wine.

I had expectations and I was suffering because I hadn't seen clearly that *everything* is just arising. Any expectation you have, even if it's spiritually correct, you have some spiritually correct expectations, Eileen—there should be loving kindness and bliss, that's all spiritually correct, but it will keep you seeking and suffering.

Look and see there is no Eileen there doing anything, and you are this witnessing presence, just watching—sometimes you'll be pleased with what you see, and sometimes you will *not* be pleased with what you see, but you'll always be the *seeing!*

Simply notice what arises. Maybe you like this, and you don't like that. There's a noticing, oh, Eileen likes this, and she doesn't like that. There are no expectations. You may have bliss arise, and it will pass. Then uncomfortable sensations and energy come through the body— and it passes. But there's no me, no 'I should' or 'I shouldn't'—I should always be blissful, I should never be angry. That goes because there's just *seeing*, and there's no one here doing it.

Of course there are preferences. You prefer things be the way you like, but that's just happening. Even the ego is happening. It's an appearance that's created by the same Mysterious Source that makes the cat meow. There's no way the ego could separate itself and create an ego. It's all from the One Mysterious Source.

Gary: Yes, what I got from Tony was being good won't get you to Heaven, and being naughty won't keep you out.

Stephen: Heaven is the absence of good and evil. The Garden of Eden is peace on Earth, prior to eating from the tree of the knowledge of good and evil. Knowing good from evil, you'll suffer all the days of your life—it's right in Genesis. The first few chapters of Genesis say it all.

Eileen: It's recognizing duality. Moving from oneness to seeing duality, and then you suffer.

Stephen: Living in the Garden of Eden doesn't mean everything is blissful, it means there's no knowledge of good and evil. There's no 'me' here who judges good and evil. The mind or the intellect is the thinking process which is the process of division, separation, judgment—knowing right and wrong, good and evil.

Exercising the intellect, knowing good from evil, we suffer all the days of our lives. So if you know good from evil, Eileen, you'll suffer. If you know bliss is good, selfishness is evil, you'll suffer. You're out of the Garden of Eden—you're kicked out. The Garden of Eden is neither good nor bad. It's before 'I', and before 'I' know good from evil. It's before 'me'—there's no I, there's no you.

Everything is just happening. You will continue searching and seeking if there are any expectations because that's the same as eating from the tree of the knowledge of good and evil. That was one of the last things that kept me going for several months. I had some negative thoughts that lasted all day long—I shouldn't be having any negative thoughts! I wanted a glass of wine, and thought, I shouldn't want any wine, I should be happy without wine. These beliefs were causing me to suffer.

[laughter]

Stephen: You're laughing! These are ideas and concepts that we've read about, or experiences we've had and we hang onto these concepts and beliefs, and we say...

Gary: That's it. That's enlightenment.

Stephen: If my beliefs and expectations are not met then something's wrong with me.

The term neti-neti is a Sanskrit term that means not this, not this. Teachers would point out that what you are is this consciousness, and questions would arise. Well, is it happiness? No, not that. Is it selfless? No, not that. Is it loving and kind? No, not that. So anything that arises is not that. So, bliss—that's not it. Bodily discomfort—that's not it. Wanting a glass of wine—nothing to do with it. Avoiding wine—that's not it.

Gary: You can't win.

Stephen: Not this, not this! It's nothing. It's nothing, this consciousness that I am. It's nothing. I was bothered for a time by these beliefs. I felt I had seen this clearly and everything was going along nicely—then I wanted a glass of wine. I still had expectations

129

and it was helpful to talk to someone to clear up the misconceptions. Everything is arising—who's doing it? There's no one doing it. Everything is arising. Everything is just happening. If you don't believe that, try to take control of your experience—and you've already done that.

Eileen: Already been there.

Stephen: Done that for years, and trying to control is the very suffering from which you're trying to be free. Trying to take control *is* the suffering. There's no one here to take control, that's why it doesn't work. Occasionally things work out, and you'll say, ahh, and you try to re-create that.

Eileen: I'm on to something, right.

Stephen: It was a coincidence.

Eileen: Yeah, see.

Gary: A coincidence arose.

Eileen: Yeah, right. I drove myself crazy trying to figure out what made the blissful experiences happen.

Stephen: Not that!

Gary: I was thinking one time that I'm a person, and there's me and there's God. I immediately saw how stupid that was because that would make me on the same level as God. Then I deduced there can only be one—there isn't anything that isn't God including me. That really saved my ass in a way because it's very egoistic to think you're as good as God.

Stephen: You'd think so, but it's egoistic to believe you have you're own separate will, but I know what you mean.

Gary: Well, there's God and there's me. If that's so, that would make me as powerful as God, and that can't be. So, there is only God, and I am That.

Eileen: But, isn't that usually seen another way? It's seen there's God, and there's this little old lowly you?

Gary: Well, I saw I had this huge ego and thought I was separate from God. That would make me really powerful if it were true. I knew I wasn't powerful like God, you know, the animating presence.

Stephen: We could say all there is, is God. This is playing with words, but, if *everything* in the universe is green, everything is green—is there any such thing as green?

Eileen: Then nothing is green, exactly.

Stephen: If everything in the universe is God, is there any such thing as God? No, there's no such thing as God. There's no God over here, and man over there. There's no God's will, or man's will.

Gary: I like what Ernest Holmes called it. He called it the *animating presence*. That works for me, the animating presence.

Eileen: There are people with different experiences they call enlightenment, right?

Gary: What Tony says, and Stephen is saying there is no one to be enlightened. So anybody who says they're enlightened, it's just conversation because there is nobody.

Eileen: Right, because what's going to be enlightened?—the body, the mind?

Gary: Who is there to be enlightened?

Stephen: The concept of enlightenment falls apart with two minutes of questioning. Who gets enlightened? Do thoughts become enlightened? Does behavior become enlightened? Does the body become enlightened? Do experiences become enlightened?

Gary: Last year I got sick and lost some of my teeth because of an infection that couldn't be stopped. For several months I was on some powerful antibiotics. Eileen gave me a book to read and it made clear to me that I was not the body. There was still pain, but it was just what arose. It was a powerful experience.

Eileen: See, that's the thing—I really do think if you are 'enlightened' you transcend everything. You're not going to get sick. Of course all these people have gotten sick and died, but you're not going to get sick, you're not going to be in pain, you're not going to have thoughts. I really do believe that, it's an image in here.

Stephen: Those images will keep you seeking and suffering.

Eileen: They're killers.

Stephen: It's neti-neti. Anything you come up with, any idea, any experience, any behavior that should be such-and-such, any feeling, any sensation, anything at all is not it—neti-neti!

There's this witnessing presence, there's this *watching* right now, Eileen, and it doesn't matter *what* it witnesses. There is awareness of whatever is here—that's it. The objects of awareness are irrelevant. There is no good and evil, no right and wrong as this consciousness that I am.

This consciousness that I am is the resolution to all spiritual seeking, and psychological suffering—this consciousness that I am. It's not a thought. It's not a behavior. It's not a belief. It's not a sensation. It's not a spiritually correct story. It's nothing. This is what I am, this witnessing presence, and it doesn't matter what I witness. I can witness pleasure or pain, health or sickness, selfishness or selfless-ness, war or peace. This is the peace that's at peace with war. This is the peace that's at peace with peace. It has nothing to do with war or peace. It's what I am, this witnessing presence.

Any idea or expectation that comes up is irrelevant. The various traditions say this in different ways. One is if you see the Buddha on the road, kill him! If you see the loving, kind, peaceful, benevolent Buddha on the road, kill him! You have these Buddha ideas, kill them all. They're useless. They won't help you, and you don't need them.

This consciousness that you are is what the ancient traditions are pointing to. This I am, this witnessing presence we all are. This is the resolution to all spiritual seeking, and psychological suffering. There is nothing to seek. There's no one to attain anything. There's just this witnessing presence that's always been here. When you were a child walking to school and kicking a rock, this consciousness was there

132

watching the little girl walk and kick the rock. It's what's witnessing this right now. You can see your feet stretched out—it sees the whole room. It doesn't matter what is seen. The objects of this consciousness are irrelevant, neti-neti. Whatever thoughts, feelings, or sensations that arise are irrelevant. This consciousness that I am is untouchable. It always is. It's what I am.

If you continue eating from the tree of the knowledge of good and evil, you'll suffer all the days of your life. When you see that tree has no value, it gets cut down and thrown away.

I am *not* this separate, controlling entity. What I am is this simple witnessing presence that's watching the show. Some of it is liked, some of it is disliked. It is what it is, and I am free of it. This freedom is not freedom to be happy, or freedom from sadness. Whatever is happening, I am neither happy nor sad. Happiness and sadness arise.

Gary: Yes, and it's really interesting.

Stephen: You wouldn't have it any other way.

Gary: It keeps unraveling. The more I see it from a neutral perspective, the less arises. It's gotten quieter. Fewer things seem to arise, which I didn't think was possible. When I don't fight with things I don't like or want, and allow them to arise, it's quieter.

Stephen: This witnessing is like people-watching when you sit on a park bench and watch people. Now you're watching Eileen. Just noticing, not making it into a practice, just noticing. Oh, look at this Eileen character with all her beliefs.

Gary: And foibles.

Stephen: You watch in amazement.

Eileen: That's crucial, not making it into a practice.

Stephen: No, just noticing. Doing a practice implies you have to attain something. You are this witnessing presence.

Gary: Already—always was and always will be.

133

Stephen: If we decide to practice meditation—this consciousness that I am is here now, and the thought arises in consciousness to meditate. So I sit down and close my eyes to meditate, and there is consciousness of sitting here with eyes closed. A half hour passes and the gong goes off signaling the end of meditation. There's consciousness of the gong and the end of the meditation.

The consciousness that I am is here before, during and after the meditation. You cannot practice or meditate yourself into this consciousness that you are. You can't get out of this consciousness that you are. It's always witnessing, watching everything that happens. Everything that happens in consciousness is irrelevant—not this, not this, neti-neti. All of your expectations are irrelevant.

Gary: One thing you said that was very good is the only thing I know is that I exist—and I thought, that's it!

Stephen: The only thing you know with absolute certainty that cannot be denied is this witnessing presence *is*. These other ideas are beliefs, concepts that were force fed to us. You had no choice about the crazy ideas of enlightenment and what it looks like. Those were fed to you.

Gary: Well, that arises, too.

Stephen: That's part of it. You can see those beliefs are happening, and then there's freedom from them. You can see all the beliefs and ideas that arise are not true. I am the *witnessing* of it all.

Gary: It's interesting how those ideas arise, it's fascinating. Where do they come from?

Stephen: Yes, how did it happen?

Gary: Isn't that far out? I just want to slap the shit out of that guy, isn't that interesting?

[laughter]

Stephen: Yes, those thoughts arise. Where did they come from?

Gary: I don't even know the guy.

Stephen: There's no me creating those thoughts.

Gary: That's tough, though, to come to the point where there's no me, I think. It's very ingrained.

Stephen: Well, the suffering brings you to that point. The suffering arises which brings about the spiritual seeking. The spiritual seeking comes to an end by seeing there's no one here doing anything. It's all an appearance. That's why we hear phrases like, nothing ever happened, there is no enlightenment, and there's no one to be enlightened. There's no one here who was ever suffering!

That's the insight that blows everything away—*not only is there no one here to be enlightened, there's no one here who was ever suffering!* There was an imaginary story playing in the head that created a disturbing energy in the body, and we label it 'suffering'. We say 'I' am suffering. There's no one who is suffering. There's an imaginary story playing that revolves around this character called Stephen, Eileen, or Gary. When the story is disturbing, an uncomfortable energy goes through the body, and we label it suffering.

Gary: And it reinforces the sense of being a separate I.

Stephen: Yes.

Gary: Tony Parsons says everyone who is searching thinks they're separate and they're trying to become one.

Stephen: Which they already are. When the searching and seeking for enlightenment is seen as a bunch of ideas that are playing as a story in the head, it's seen as imagination, it's seen there is no one who was ever suffering, there's no one who can be enlightened—it was all imagination.

Gary: What we are was never born, and can never die.

Stephen: This awareness that I am. This Universal Life that we are. These particular forms pass, the Universal Presence creates another form, and life goes on.

Eileen: But there's no time. Without time we don't have a story. Thought creates time, and the story. The story can only exist in time.

Stephen: That's why it's I AM, not I was, or I will be. I AM the way. Not I *was* or I *will be* the way. *I am* the way, the truth and the life—I AM.

Who has not found the heaven below
Will fail of it above
God's residence is next to mine
His furniture is love
—Emily Dickinson

32

That's Interesting!—Now Throw It Away

Eileen: Buddhists meditate, but what happened to Buddha was when he gave up meditating, right? So do you meditate in order to give it up? It's like when somebody wins the lottery and you say, what time did you buy the ticket? Was it a Wednesday night, and which store? What were you thinking? You can re-create what the person did, but you're not going to win the lottery.

Stephen: That implies some event is going to happen.

Eileen: An event.

Stephen: What's being pointed out is not an event. It's here prior to an event happening, during the event, and after the event. It's this witnessing presence, this watching. It seems to me that's what the ancient traditions are pointing to, and it's what I'm talking about.

Gary: There's nothing going on.

Stephen: If you're waiting for an event, any event will have a beginning and an end. What's being pointed out is this consciousness we already are—it's just watching.

Eileen: But we hear about events all the time. I heard about someone who got enlightened when he was fourteen years old in math class. He knew all the answers, yet he hadn't studied. He could no longer go on with his regular life. He went to see Yogananda, and then Ramana. When he was younger he had dreams of Ramana standing over his crib. He didn't know who it was at the time, but when he met Ramana, he knew this was the guy who was in his room with him as a baby. There seems to be a before and after. At fourteen years of age there was an experience from which he couldn't go back. He was transformed. Do you see my problem? He was transformed. From then on it was a different story. Yes, he spent years with Ramana, and all that kind of stuff.

Stephen: What was *not* transformed?

We can see what was transformed—his experience, his behavior, the energy in the body may have been different—all of that may have been transformed. But, what was *not* transformed? What I am pointing out is what was *not* transformed.

It's always here—this witnessing. There's no awakening of this consciousness we are. You can remember back to any point in time throughout your life history, there's always been this watching happening. This watching is this consciousness, this witnessing—it's what we are. Without it, nothing exists. It's always been here. So this consciousness doesn't wake up. This consciousness doesn't have any enlightenment experiences. This consciousness doesn't go through any drastic changes.

Eileen: It doesn't go through any changes.

Stephen: No, and this is what's being pointed out. If we refer to and recall interesting stories of enlightenment, awakening, and transformational experiences...

Eileen: They're all very interesting experiences.

Stephen: They're interesting, but throw them away! They don't have anything to do with what you already are—this witnessing presence that you can sense right now! If you get caught up in the stories and expectations, you'll continue suffering and seeking.

Gary: There is a palpable difference between an apparent individual who has the egoic point of view of I.

Stephen: There is.

Gary: And then has the realization or the knowledge that he doesn't exist as a separate entity.

Stephen: I agree.

Gary: It's a very different kind of feeling—there's a very different individual, apparently.

Stephen: In the appearance as a person—the body/mind organism.

Gary: The way they operate, apparently there's a change.

Stephen: But as soon as we look to the Buddha, or we look to any other individual who appears to be living with the absence of 'I' and say, well, what happened to you? What's your story? And we try to re-create it, we're caught up in the story. If I can do what you did, or if this happens to me then I'll get it. That's missing what's being pointed to, which is the watching, and it's already here.

Gary: Yes, you went to see someone, so if I go see him, maybe that will be the event that does it for me, because it did it for you, apparently.

Stephen: Right, so there's the assumption that something happened. But, nothing ever happened. What was seen is the whole story of psychological suffering is just a story. So everything gets thrown out— the story of suffering, and the story of enlightenment.

There is in truth no cause, no result, and no action; all that is illusory.
There is no world and no dweller in it.
—Ramana Maharshi

33

Fighting—Surrendering—Forgiving

Stephen: It's really simple, and it brought an end to the spiritual seeking and psychological suffering. I saw there is no one—there is no Stephen who was ever suffering. There is no psychological suffering other than a story playing in the head with disturbing images that create disturbing sensations in the body—that's it.

Gary: In fact, that was just stuff arising.

Stephen: Right, and it was just happening.

Gary: And you didn't like what arose.

Stephen: Right.

Gary: If you responded by saying, that's interesting, and being happy is interesting, the suffering falls away.

Stephen: Yes, that's the way we come into the world.

Gary: But we have preferences, we like this and don't like that.

Stephen: Yes, and the 'I' develops, which is the sense of being separate and in control. 'I' create the happiness or sadness. So this 'I' is questioned, who am I?

Gary: Everybody I work with tells me stories about how 'I' did this, that, and the other thing. Every time they tell me a story about having a bad time with someone—I say, do you see it just arose? They have a point of view about it and they're not neutral about what arose. First of all, they think they're doing things. Secondly, they have a point of view about what arose—they don't like it, they don't want it.

Eileen: They feel responsible for it.

Gary: They think if they're good they're going to heaven, and if they do something bad, they'll be kept out of heaven.

Eileen: That's the sense of being a controlling entity. If you believe you are a controlling entity, then you're responsible for everything that happens.

Stephen: Yes, so is there any separate, controlling entity there? If there's not, then you're suffering over a belief, an imagined entity that doesn't exist. So you look and you can't find one.

Gary: It's like being afraid of the boogey man.

Stephen: Yes, so you turn the light on, and there's no one there. A relaxation happens when you turn the light on. If you're sleeping and you hear a loud noise downstairs, you run downstairs thinking someone has broken into your home. You get downstairs and turn the light on and you see the wind knocked a vase onto the floor. So you were suffering over something that doesn't exist.

Gary: What seems to be happening is that being really tough on herself arises. Things like expectations of perfection, and being meticulous in cleaning—that's what arises for her. It doesn't seem like she sees that as arising, but it's something she must do. So I see suffering around that.

Stephen: Yes, that's the story of suffering. It's a misconception, an unexamined belief in the existence of a separate Eileen. But, Eileen's will is the will of God. Whatever's happening is not your creation, it's just happening. Seeing this, there's a new perspective and it's like the analogy of believing there's a burglar in your house. You're suffering while coming down the stairs, there's a disturbing energy in the body, and you're wondering how many burglars are there? But there's no one there! There's no burglar there. God moved the wind and knocked over the vase. There was a belief that a burglar was in your home.

The same is true with psychological suffering. There's a belief in a separate, controlling entity there which is at the root of all psychological suffering—believing I am this separate, controlling entity. So we look and we see there's none here. Not only do we find nothing, but we cannot *exercise* control. That's the practical way to see this—if I do exist as a separate, controlling entity, then go ahead and exercise control. Then you try, and you notice that everything just arises, it just happens—whether I want it or not. Well, I've said I don't want anger anymore; I don't want any negative thoughts. I've made a conscious decision—no more negative thoughts, no more anger—and then they arise anyway!

There's no separate, controlling entity here. So if I am not the separate, controlling entity I thought I was my whole life, then what am I? The only thing about yourself, if you notice in your own experience, which cannot be denied, is that you are this consciousness, this witnessing—this is what I am. I am the witnessing. What should I do? I watch. I witness. I observe. That's it. There's nothing to do.

Eileen: There's nothing to do.

Gary: Right.

Eileen: It's an attachment to a false idea.

Stephen: Yes, and what happens is seeing there's no one *here* doing anything, it's immediately seen there's no one *there*, and there's no one *there*. Most of our lives there was a belief that I, this person, is responsible for its actions.

Eileen: Then you hold other people responsible.

Stephen: Seeing there's no one *here*, immediately it's seen there's no one *there*. So whatever happens—Gary may be kind and pleasant...

Gary: Whatever arises in Gary.

Stephen: ...or he may be obnoxious. But there's no sense he is personally doing anything. It's just happening. I may say, get out of here, Gary, you're being obnoxious, but it's not him personally.

Gary: Right, it's just arising.

Stephen: Yes, if the dog comes in here and bites us, we'll kick the dog out of here. We know it's not a personal matter. This is forgiveness. It's seen there's no one to forgive, so this natural forgiveness happens.

Surrendering happens because it's seen there's no one here doing anything. There's no one who surrenders—it's not 'I' surrender. It's realized there's never been anyone here doing anything. So the energy that was going into the 'I should and I shouldn't, and I need to control', that energy of resistance falls away because it's seen there's no one here doing anything. There's a surrendering that happens—a surrendering to *what is*. There's a surrendering to whatever arises. Not that 'I' surrender, it's just seen that my whole life I've been fighting a war with an unloaded weapon. This weapon called 'me' has no power. So surrendering happens.

Come now, and let us reason together, saith the LORD: though your sins be as scarlet, they shall be as white as snow; though they be red like crimson, they shall be as wool. —**The Book of Isiah**

34

Willow Trees and Egos Happen

Stephen: It's a challenge to persuade someone who is absolutely convinced they are in control of everything that's happening in their life, and they're doing everything! Because of the belief they have of themselves, it's projected onto others.

Gary: Right.

Stephen: That's fine, it's part of the play.

Gary: That's what arises.

Stephen: Yes, it's fine. I have no interest in convincing anyone.

Gary: Everyone is that already.

Stephen: Even the ego, the sense of being me, is an expression of the One Mysterious Source—the same as the apparent person who has no sense of ego. It's the same Mysterious Source expressing itself as an oak tree, a pine tree, a willow tree. A willow tree goes with the flow of the wind, a pine tree will snap. Is a willow tree better than a pine tree? They're all an expression of the One. The ego is an expression of the One.

Gary: Yes.

Stephen: And you say, wow, look at the ego! Look at the One Mysterious Source express itself as an ego. We know what that's like—and there's nothing wrong with it.

Gary: No.

Stephen: There's really nothing wrong with that.

Gary: It's how it must be.

Stephen: It just is—wow! It's a different play of life as a 'me' compared to the absence of me. There's a different experience. They're both enjoyable. It can be just as enjoyable to be caught up in the sense of ego because you have the extreme swings of gratification when you succeed, and the dejection when you fail—I did it! I lost it! I did it! Wow! That continues, now it's just witnessed. I am the witnessing presence of this Stephen character. This Stephen character is the personality based on its biology and conditioning. So that's just happening.

All the world's a stage,
And all the men and women merely players.
They have their exits and their entrances,
And one man in his time plays many parts.
—William Shakespeare

35

Self-Realization, Awakening & Enlightenment?

Diana: Is it unfair to ask, as I have not read your book, what do you think is Self-realization, or are you going to tell me to read the book?

[Laughter]

Stephen: That's the question I wrote in the book, *The Outrageous Myths of Enlightenment*, "What are self-realization, awakening, liberation and enlightenment?" So that's the question most people have who are seeking spiritually.

Diana: So, can I ask you now?

Stephen: Well, I can ask you that question and we can talk about it. If you're interested, then we can see. What you may find is that what you're seeking, what self-realization is, what awakening is, what enlightenment is—it's what you already are. You can hear this and say, okay, I agree—but it's conceptual.

Diana: Right.

Stephen: When you are really suffering, you're at the end of your rope and you feel you can't take it anymore, then you find out. That was my experience. I don't know if that's necessary. You just can't take it anymore. You can't take living as a separate person and you're ready to kill yourself—I was at certain points.

Then you'll find out what self-realization is, what awakening is, and what enlightenment is—you'll find out there isn't any. It's seen there is no such thing as enlightenment, and there is no person who can be enlightened. There's no separate entity.

All suffering comes out of this sense of being separate. You're a separate person and you're not good enough, there's something wrong with you—so you're suffering. When it gets to a certain point the realization can happen that all suffering stems from this sense of being separate—a separate person who has to make her own way in the world, and it's not easy. So we turn to different approaches, and we go down different paths in our life. Because it doesn't feel quite right, something feels wrong. There's the sense that something is wrong with me. Something is wrong with me, and something is wrong with the world.

The ancient traditions point to the fact that at the root of all suffering is the sense of being separate—separate from our fellow man, separate from God, separate from everything. Being a separate entity and having to fight, struggle, kick and scratch our way through this life. It's not easy living like that. So we read about the fact that the end of spiritual seeking and psychological suffering comes when we see we're not separate, there is no separate person here.

Diana: But how do you see that? The only way to see that is to experience it.

Stephen: Well, the spiritual literature says that at the root of suffering is this sense of being a separate person, and we notice that in our own experience. We notice, well, let me see if it's true in my own experience—is my suffering happening when I feel I'm separate? In other words we look into what's happening when we're suffering.

Lenny: What is your experience? Without reading about it what is your personal experience?

Stephen: My experience of suffering?

Lenny: Yes, without talking about what you read. What is your personal experience?

Stephen: The suffering brought me to the point where I was willing to look into some fundamental questions. The fundamental questions are—what am I? Is there a separate entity here? The spiritual traditions say there is no separate entity here, and the sense of being a separate person is at the root of all suffering. So the suggestion is to look in your own experience and see if that's true. Is there any separate entity here?

Lenny: And what did you find out?

Stephen: For me the suggestion was to look and see if there's any separate entity here. So you question that, and you say who do I feel I am? Who is Stephen? Who is Lenny? Who am I? When you say,

Lenny, what do you mean?

Lenny: I'm asking about you.

Stephen: Right, well, I don't want this to be only about me. This was beneficial for me so I want you to look, too—because this is not only about me and my experience. It's about both of us—it's about all of us.

When I looked in my experience and asked who is Stephen? Who do I feel I am? I felt I was in control. I am the controller of Stephen's life. If you ask me, who is Stephen? I am the one who's in control of Stephen and his life. I'm in control of his thoughts and I'm responsible for his thoughts. I'm in control of his feelings, his sensations, his relationships, his career—Stephen. I'm the one who's in control of making sure my life experience works out. Making sure I'm happy most of the time, and I avoid sadness. That's who I felt I was. That's the sense of ego, the sense of being a separate, controlling entity, a separate person who must take control of his life experience.

Ramana suggests this and many others—find out who you are. Who am I? This was the process for me. Looking into and questioning, who is Stephen? I could feel an energy here in the chest and stomach. It's an uncomfortable energy. It's an energy of resistance. Resisting what I don't like, and trying to grasp onto what I do like. So it's a sense and a belief that I'm in control of my experience. I'm a separate entity who can control his own experience—control his thoughts, his feelings, sensations, actions, relationships, and career—the whole package. So this is who I felt I was.

So now I'm questioning that. What is this energy of resistance? What is it based on? Is there any separate, controlling entity here? Is there any separate person here? The ancient traditions say there isn't one. They say if you see there isn't a separate entity here, and all is one, then there's a sense of relief that happens.

This resistance that I felt I was, this ego, you can feel it in your stomach, in your chest, in your neck. It's a sense of resistance to what is. You want to resist the unpleasant experiences, and grasp onto the pleasant. You want the good, and you don't want the bad. And there's a 'me' here, an ego who wants to do that.

If there's a belief that there's a separate person here who can control his experience, then it's questioned. We look and we see, well, if there is an ego, if there is a separate entity here who can exercise control, if this ego I believe I am has any power, then it should be able to exercise control, right? It should be able to control thoughts,

148

feelings, sensations, and actions. If there is any separate, controlling entity, any separate ego here, it should be able to take control of his life, shouldn't it?

Either I'm in control or I'm not. It's black and white, there's no gray. There isn't just a *little bit* of control. If there's one little part you're not in control, then there is no control. Either there is a controlling entity or person here or there isn't. It's not a little bit. It's not that I can control *this*, but I can't control *that*.

So I'm looking into this uncomfortable energy of resistance which is the ego, and I'm questioning it. Does it have any substance? Is it real? Or is it just based on a belief? If it's real, I should be able to exercise control, shouldn't I? If the ego, this sense of being a separate person has any power then I should be able to exercise control over thoughts, shouldn't I?—and feelings, sensations, actions, behavior, all of that. If I am a separate, controlling entity, shouldn't I be able to exercise control over my experience? Yes?

So I sit here and I notice thoughts just happen. Try to take control of your thoughts—go ahead and do it. You may be successful for a short period of time, and then something will come in and disturb that seemingly successful period of control. So I'm sitting here and I'm questioning this ego. Can I control thoughts? No. Why would you ever have a negative thought at all? If you could control your thoughts, take control right now, and have only positive thoughts. What are you waiting for? Why would you wait? Thoughts happen. If you don't believe that, then go ahead and take control of your thoughts. Good luck.

So I notice in my own experience there's no separate entity here creating or controlling thoughts—thoughts happen! Positive thoughts, negative thoughts, whatever you want to call them, they just happen. Where do they come from? I don't know. Is Stephen controlling any thoughts? I tried for quite a while to have only positive thoughts, it doesn't work. So there's no separate ego here controlling thoughts.

What about feelings?—happiness, sadness or any feeling. If there's a separate entity here who can exercise control, then I'll be able to control my feelings, and have only joy and happiness, and never have anger or sadness. So let's see if I can exercise control. If there is an ego here, a separate entity with any capacity to control, surely it can exercise control. Then why am I waiting? Why don't I go ahead and have only joy all the time? So, happiness and sadness, joy and anger—feelings just arise, they just happen. If you don't believe that, then take control of your feelings now! What are you waiting for? Don't wait

149

until next week. So I found there is no separate entity who can control thoughts. There's no separate entity who can control feelings.

What about sensations in the body? I want only pleasure, I don't want pain. Why would I want pain? Is there any separate entity who can exercise control over sensations? If there is, why are we waiting? Why don't we exercise control now and have only pleasure? Would you ever have pain if you had control over the sensations in your body? Why would you choose pain?

There are thoughts, feelings, and sensations—that's the general experience we humans have. Then there are actions and behaviors. And we ask, what about my behavior or my actions? If there is any separate, controlling entity here, I should be able to control my behavior and actions. My actions and behavior should only be loving and kind! I should be loving, kind and peaceful all the time. I should never be angry or selfish. I should never have any negative behavior or actions. I should never yell at anyone. I should always be thoughtful and generous, loving, peaceful, kind, and compassionate—if I'm in control, right?

So, we look for a controlling entity because we believe there is a separate person who can exercise control. This is the energy you feel in your stomach and chest. This is the energy of resistance and trying to control. You can feel it, it's uncomfortable. So what is it trying to control? It's trying to control thoughts, feelings, sensations, actions and behaviors. Isn't that the human experience in general? We have thoughts, feelings, sensations, actions, and behaviors.

Diana: The suffering is resisting.

Stephen: Yes. So we notice at the root of psychological suffering, and we feel it in our own experience, is this energy of resistance—I like this, I don't like that, and trying to control.

Lenny: I was thinking it's also about how we are taught to see what is good and what is bad. Like pain is bad. This is how we're taught, it's not because we choose to see things that way.

Diana: It's conditioning.

Lenny: It's conditioning. Because if you are able to accept everything the way it is, there is no more suffering. There's no more resistance.

Stephen: We want to get to the root of this, because the way you put it, there's one key we want to focus on, you said, "If *you* are able to accept," if *Lenny* is able to accept, if *Diana* is able to accept.

Lenny: If you surrender.

Stephen: If YOU surrender! We want to look into this YOU, Lenny. Is Lenny able to accept, is Jason able to accept, is Charles able to accept, is Diana able to accept, is Stephen able to accept? Who is this *you* that is able to accept?

Lenny: It's an image of what I think I am.

Stephen: Can the image you have of yourself do anything at all? This makes it personal when you look in your own experience and ask, is Lenny able to control? We want to get to the root of this. So in this investigation of 'who am I?' we notice this resistance, this ego. We question it and recognize that everything is happening—thoughts, feelings, sensations, actions—it's all happening. Even resistance is just happening. This uncomfortable energy is just happening. I'm not doing that, it's just happening.

I thought I was this Stephen character, a controlling entity. In this investigation, this observation, looking into this it's seen there's no one here. How do I see this? Because I thought I was controlling thoughts. I thought Stephen was in control of thoughts, and it's seen that thoughts just arise, they just happen. So where is Stephen? What's Stephen's role in the thinking process if thoughts just arise? Is Stephen the thinker? If I am the thinker, then I should be able to exercise control over thoughts. I can't do it! So, Stephen is not the thinker. There's no thinker here. Then you check all of your experience— thoughts, feelings, sensations, actions, behaviors, and you look for the one who's doing them and you find nothing, no one!

Lenny: You could say Stephen is the body.

Stephen: It's a label. There is no psychological suffering for the body. It's only this image of me, Stephen, who can suffer psychologically. The resistance comes about because of the assumption based on the unexamined belief in the existence of a separate entity, a separate ego called, Stephen.

When it's seen there's no Stephen here, and thoughts happen,

151

feelings happen, sensations happen, actions happen. There's no Stephen here. I am not the separate entity I thought I was, so, what am I? My entire life that's who I thought I was—this energy of resistance. I'm the one who's in control, and it's seen I am not that, there's nothing here, there's nothing here!

I've seen that through this investigation. And I've confirmed it by trying to *exercise* control. You say, okay, I don't find any controlling entity here, but maybe I've overlooked it. So I'm going to make this investigation practical, and ask can I *exercise* control? If there's an entity here in each of us that has any separate power, surely it can exercise that power! So I'm making this investigation practical.

Diana: I understand. I understand the thoroughness of the investigation. Now is that something you've experienced?—the non-existence of the controlling entity? Like the way you experience pleasure? Or the way the form has experienced pleasure or pain. It was helpful for me to hear your presentation of the investigation, I enjoyed that. But my next question is have you had an experience, because you are still in form. So this form has or has not had the experience of no-separation?

Stephen: The first part of the investigation is based on looking into this separate entity.

Diana: I understood that, and it's clear.

Stephen: The second part will answer your question. All my life I thought I was this ego.

Diana: Right, right, right.

Stephen: It's clearly seen there's no one here.

Diana: Right, I understood that totally.

Stephen: The next question is, if I am not the ego I thought I was my entire life, then what am I?

Diana: Okay, that's still not answering my question, that's in between.

Stephen: We'll get there.

152

Diana: Okay.

Stephen: What I am is the peace you're talking about, it *is* the absence of separation you're talking about—what *I am*. Seeing through what I am *not*, the sense of separation falls away.

Diana: Right.

Stephen: What's left? What's left is what's always been here.

Diana: Right.

Stephen: This will answer your question, stay with me. I know what you mean. Just go along with me. Because there is no one who experiences the absence of separation. There's no one to experience the bliss. There's no one to experience the peace. See, it's not for a someone! The question, 'Have you experienced the absence of separation?' is based on a premise that there is someone here to experience the absence of separation—see how that doesn't work? The question comes from the perspective of a person who wants to...

Diana: No, it comes from, well, we are still in form here.

Stephen: There is no one in form. The question is based on the premise that there's a person here, and there are separate forms. That's going through the mind. There's no separation until you think, until the intellect is exercised.

I want to talk about what we are. Your questions are all going through the mind. There's no separate form. There's no separate person who experiences the absence of ego. There's no separate person who experiences bliss. There's no separate person who can be enlightened. There's no separate person. There's no separate form! If we remove one atom of hydrogen from the water molecules in your body it will fall apart.

Diana: Yes, but that keeps it together, that one molecule.

Stephen: Without thought there is no separate form. We're going through the mind and trying to see that all is one, and the mind is the tool of division.

153

Diana: Right.

Stephen: We're using the tool of division to understand that all is one. We can't do it. And to experience oneness—can't do it. The mind is the tool of division, the tool of separation, the tool that labels me and you, form and spirit. That's the tool we're using to see that all is one.

Diana: Do we have a different tool?

Stephen: That's the tool we humans use. But there is no 'we' who has any tool. The universe is expressing itself. I know what you're talking about and I'm trying to chip away at answering your question.

I want to talk about what we are. My interest is in sharing the fact that it's possible to be free of spiritual seeking, and free of psychological suffering. I stick with the fundamentals of what we are, and what we are not. Through this recognition there is a relief from the seeking and psychological suffering. Then you'll have a new perspective on your ideas of experiencing the oneness, and all the ideas that come up. You'll have a new perspective. It'll be a perspective from the sense of the fact that you are this awareness that's watching everything that's happening, so there's a new perspective. You'll notice these concepts and questions that come up are much less important. You'll see the questions don't even matter because you're at peace, and it doesn't matter what questions come up.

Diana: Questions that come up are like what?

Stephen: The questions are mental noise. They have nothing to do with the peace you really want. There's the sense if I get my questions answered, then I'll live in peace. What we really want is this sense of peace, the sense of love, the sense that everything is okay.

We go down different paths, and we have all these questions. We think if I get my questions answered then I'll have the peace, the sense of relief, the sense that everything is okay. But you'll notice getting your questions answered has nothing to do with the peace you really want. You'll notice the questions are noise in the background. But *you* are the peace.

I want to talk about what we are. There's no separate entity here, so what am I? There's one question, who am I? There are two sides to that question. One side is seeing what you are *not*, which is a separate ego, because that's at the root of psychological suffering, the sense of

154

being separate. So it's seen through this investigation there is no separate entity here. That's seeing what I am *not*.

If I'm not this separate person, this separate entity, then what am I? What is it about us that's always here and has always been here? It's never changed—it's always been witnessing, watching. It's this awareness, this consciousness.

This consciousness that we are has always been here. This consciousness that I am watches thoughts come up, it witnesses questions that come up. It witnesses the question, who am I? It witnesses the silence when there are no questions. It witnesses the happiness and the sadness. It was aware of the body when we were younger, and it's aware as we get older. The body was young, and it's getting older, but the consciousness is still the same.

You remember when you were a child, the consciousness looking out at the body, and the body looks different now, but the consciousness is the same as when we were little children. It's this looking, this seeing. It's aware of everything in this room right now. It's aware of these words. It's aware of the thoughts that are arising in response to these words. You hear these words and then thoughts arise in response—there is awareness of that. This awareness has always been here. It has to be here. It's primary. It's essential. It's what you are in essence. It's what we all are in essence—this awareness, this witnessing presence that's just watching. It's not something you can do—this awareness—it just is. So we notice this seeing is happening, this awareness is happening—it's just happening. It's what I am. It's what you are. And it's watching all of this. It's aware of everything in the room—this awareness that we are. It's very peaceful. There are no problems with it.

Diana: Yes.

Stephen: This is what I am.

Diana: I understand that. I am aware of that. I experience that.

Stephen: It's pretty nice—this awareness.

Diana: Yes.

Stephen: This is what we are—this awareness. There are no problems. Problems are in thinking, and thinking based on a belief that 'I' am in

155

control of my experience. There's no one here, there's only awareness. That's what I am. What do I do? I watch. I just watch.

Diana: What is the content of your everyday experience? Where does that come from?

Stephen: It's a mystery. Where do thoughts, feelings, and sensations come from?

Diana: No, just the experience.

Stephen: Where does my experience come from?

Diana: Yes, are you waiting for everyday to present its mystery, or what's your input?

Stephen: Well, we're all the same in essence. The same is true for you. It's not possible that we're different. I didn't attain anything. No one attains anything.

Diana: I understand that, but I'm asking about your daily experience, what informs your everyday life?

Stephen: What I am is this watching, this witnessing presence is what I am.

Diana: I understand that.

Stephen: So, what does this witnessing presence do? What is the experience of this witnessing presence? It witnesses, it watches.

Diana: But, you do something everyday.

Stephen: I don't do anything.

Diana: Okay, you don't do anything.

Stephen: Everything happens. From the perspective of what I am—I watch. That's what I am. I am this witnessing presence, and so are you.

Diana: Right.

Stephen: That's what you do, too—you watch. That's the only thing you've ever done, everything else has happened. Do you create the oak trees, and the grass, and the flowers—do you do that?

Diana: No, but that doesn't help me understand what I'm asking you.

Stephen: Do you create your thoughts?

Diana: More and more I witness my thoughts. But I am asking you a specific question.

Stephen: Everything is happening, that's my experience. Everything is happening. I'm not doing anything.

Diana: You're not doing your work, you're not...

Stephen: Oh, I work. Work happens. See, there's a difference when it's seen there's no one here doing it. You're asking me what do I do, and from an absolute perspective of what I am—I watch. I watch this Stephen character work, eat, feed the cats, and clean the house.

Diana: So that's your experience of life?

Stephen: I watch these thoughts happen. I watch these meetings happen. I hear these words happening. Who's doing it? Who is creating these words?

Diana: So, that's your experience, you're not there?

Stephen: I am the witnessing presence, and so are you!

Diana: I understand that. Is that your experience?

Stephen: The question is based on a false premise—what is your experience? There's no 'I'. See, that's the whole point. There's just consciousness witnessing. If you want to know what I am doing—I am witnessing. That's what I am.

Diana: So you're witnessing your pleasure, and witnessing your pain.

Stephen: Yes, and so are you.

Diana: Well, you can't speak for me because you don't know. Ask me, please. Theoretically you are assuming that's my experience, but practically that may not be my experience. That's what I was trying to ask you, if that's your experience. Because I understand conceptually that's the truth, but whether we are there is another question. If you are telling me that's what I'm experiencing, I'm going to say, no! That's a concept. I experience that some of the time, witnessing my experience. But, no, I can't say that's my experience.

Jason: You see it when you don't witness, too, is that what you're saying? Do you notice when you're not witnessing?

Diana: What I'm saying is I'm not in that place where I am witnessing all the time.

Jason: How do you know that?

Diana: I feel it! It's not a matter of knowing—that's how I know, by feeling. I understand what you are talking about, but my experience is I still experience pleasure and pain. The more I deepen my experience of who I am really, the more I can witness some of it, but it's not a permanent experience. That's where I draw my information about who I am, it's from my experience. That experience is deepening maybe, of who I am, truly. But I'm not there all the time.

Jason: Who sees that you're not there all the time?

Diana: It's not a matter of who. I understand the question, but I don't experience that! I understand all of the concepts you've presented so wonderfully.

Jason: You say sometimes you're witnessing and sometimes you're not—when you're not witnessing, you're noticing that though, aren't you? You just mentioned sometimes you are, and sometimes you're not, right?

Diana: When I'm not witnessing, am I aware of that? Yes.

Jason: You must be.

Stephen: I'll speak from my own experience, I felt that, too. I thought

158

there were flip-flops from witnessing to being identified with the person and the thoughts. I thought there was a flip-flop. What I realized is the witnessing is always happening, this consciousness is always happening, whether the sense of a flip-flop happens or not. There's always a 'seeing' of it. There's always a witnessing of it. The false sense of a flip-flop was based on a belief that if I know myself as this consciousness, as this awareness, then my experience will meet certain expectations—there will be peace all the time, loving-kindness all the time, there will never be anger, I'll have only positive thoughts—those were beliefs I had.

Diana: That's something different.

Stephen: What happened to me for a while, and I thought it was a problem, I thought I was losing this consciousness or this awareness because negative thoughts would arise, and I thought, well, I shouldn't be having any negative thoughts if I really saw this. If I really knew myself as consciousness I wouldn't have negative thoughts.

Diana: But everything is in this consciousness including negative thoughts.

Stephen: Right, even the sense of ego.

Diana: Right.

Stephen: For a while there was a belief that I lost it. Because I believed I shouldn't be having this disturbing energy, I shouldn't be having negative thoughts. There should be peaceful, loving kindness all the time. But that's not what's being pointed out. What's being pointed out is what I am. I am the witnessing of it. And the witnessing of it is never gone. The awareness or the consciousness that I am is always witnessing, it's always watching, it's always seeing, it's always aware of the sensations in the body, it's always aware. It's what I am in essence, it's primary.

If there is no awareness or consciousness, there can't be any belief in a flip-flop, there can't be any uncomfortable energy—there can't be any sensations without this awareness. For a while I had these beliefs that if I really knew that I am this awareness, then my experience—thoughts, feelings, sensations and all of that would meet these certain criteria. If I wasn't happy, peaceful, blissful, calm, loving and kind all

159

the time, then I lost it. And it's seen that what I am is the witnessing presence that's watching my experience go from loving, peaceful and kind, and then flipping to the ugliness of the ego. But I was always there watching it.

Diana: The ego is not even ugly. It's just different colors of the same consciousness. That's a judgment

Stephen: Yes, right. I'm using words to describe the experience.

Lenny: We can say it's aliveness. All those things happen, judging, the pain, all those things happen.

Charles: Well, I really get that thoughts happen. I'm getting them almost constantly and there's awareness of them, and the emotions, too. But my actions—I hit a wall with that because my actions are more concrete.

Stephen: Right, that's very common. If you follow your actions back, what usually happens prior to an action? In most cases, unless it's a reflex, aren't most actions preceded by thoughts, feelings, or sensations? Someone may say something about Charles and you get offended by it. So a response happens and maybe you strike back. And you say, well, I should be in control of my actions. But isn't it true that actions are preceded by thoughts, feelings and sensations? And then an action follows—isn't that the case?

Charles: Well, what about other decisions you think out, like whether I should loan money to someone, or whether I should put a new roof on the house, or buy a new car—things like that. These are things you think out rationally, supposedly, and then you take action.

Stephen: Right, so if you follow any action, even an action like that, making a decision to put a new roof on the house, or should I buy a new car? If you follow it back, a thought or a series of thoughts happen, and an action follows. Isn't that the case? Every action that happens in my experience, other than a biological reflex, involves thought—thoughts happen and then actions follow. So where is the actor? Where's the thinker? Is there any entity creating the thoughts? Is there any actor creating the actions? Or is thinking happening, and acting happening? It seems to me that everything is happening, even

160

the actions. There's nothing that isn't simply *happening*.

Charles: It's more difficult to avoid psychological pain during the decision making process when you have to make a decision that affects someone else. It seems you can't avoid the psychological pain that's there.

Stephen: Well, what if you see there's no Charles? There's no separate Charles creating the thoughts. There's no separate Charles creating the feelings. There's no separate Charles creating the sensations. There's no separate Charles creating the actions. So, what is Charles' role in the decision making process? What is Charles' role?

Is there any Charles there to take credit if things work out well for everyone involved? Is there any Charles there to take the blame if things don't work out well? Is there any Charles there? Is there any Charles there who can suffer? Do you see how the recognition that there is no separate Charles there resolves all psychological suffering, and spiritual seeking? All psychological suffering and spiritual seeking are from the point of view of a separate Charles. What if there is no Charles? If you are not Charles, then what are you? You are the witnessing presence of Charles and all the actions that happen. That's who I am—who you are. There's no separate entity there.

Lenny: This is still a belief, am I right? It's still a belief?

Stephen: What is still a belief?

Lenny: That you are awareness.

Diana: Or there's no one there.

Lenny: It's still a belief. It's not...

Diana: ...an experience.

Lenny: Right, it's not an experience. It's something you got through the mind using the mind as a tool and it's still a belief, it's not an experience.

Diana: What drives your actions? People may have a thought to take a certain action. All sorts of thoughts come to mind, and there's no one

161

there, according to what I understand, and then you act on the thoughts. What makes the discernment there between taking certain actions like should I climb up a tree or should I go to work today? There are many choices. If no one is there, then thoughts happen and there is action and nobody is responsible. That is my question, what drives the actions and choices in your life?

Stephen: The same thing that drives you. What's the source of the universe? What's the source of an oak tree?

Lenny: I don't know?

Stephen: It's a mystery.

Diana: Yes, but I can't talk about something I don't experience. I'm not experiencing that mystery. I'm experiencing the beginning of the day...

Lenny: Even 'mystery' is a concept.

Stephen: Everything we're talking about is a concept in order to put it into words. If we see it's all concepts, then you are free of the concepts.

Diana: No, you can't see unless you experience it.

Lenny: Exactly.

Diana: Unless you experience something, you can't really see it. It can help to see the concepts.

Stephen: Okay, well, I'll stick to the basics because there are a lot of different questions that arise, and for me they were all resolved. There are an infinite number of questions we can ask.

Diana: That's why I'm asking you a specific personal question that might help us understand. What drives your actions and choices during your day? As much as you know the concept there is no Stephen, and you are watching everything, still everyday you are involved in this form, and you are participating in various activities. So I am asking you, what determines your choices in your daily experience?

Stephen: How would I know? It's a mystery. What makes an oak tree an oak tree?

Diana: I think you do know, because you must have an experience.

Stephen: The only experience I can speak of is that I am witnessing.

Diana: That's your only experience.

Stephen: That's my experience.

Diana: So you are completely detached from everything that's happening?

Stephen: No! There's no one here who's detached! From the perspective of a separate me, which is a false premise, all these questions arise. Like what is your experience? There's just witnessing! I'm trying to answer a question based on a false premise.

Diana: So you can't answer because you are so identified with awareness, who you truly are.

Stephen: No! There's no one who's identified. There's just one—consciousness. You say, answer my question! And the question is, what time is purple? I can't answer that question because it's based on a false premise! Regarding your other questions the false premise is there is some separate entity who has an experience. Some separate entity who can be identified or detached. My experience is I am this witnessing presence watching the show, and the show happens.

Diana: You're watching the show. So how do you answer his question as far as making choices that involve other people?

Stephen: This witnessing presence that I am...

Diana: But he's not there. He's not experiencing what you're experiencing.

Stephen: I can only answer from my own perspective, and the realization that we're all the same in essence.

Diana: So the moment we understand theoretically that we are all witnessing...

Stephen: There are two sides to it. What you are is the witnessing presence, and you are *not* a separate entity.

Diana: Right, so the moment I understand that fully...

Stephen: We could say, 'see' that.

Diana: See that fully, then I'm free of suffering and then...

Stephen: There's a new perspective, I'll put it that way. Because if I believe that I am Stephen...

Diana: I understand that thoroughly. So if I understand that thoroughly I'll be free of suffering and I'll be self-realized?

Stephen: There's no one who's self-realized!

Diana: Well, I have to ask the question from where I am. I mean the fact that Stephen is not here is your experience, but it's not mine.

Stephen: Then my suggestion to you is the same that was made to me, and the suggestion is to look and see if you are a separate entity. Is there a separate Diana there?

Diana: Yeah, I asked that question many times.

Stephen: That's what I suggest because if it's seen in your own experience—who is this Diana you feel you are? Who is this? Who is Diana really? Who is it that I feel I am. I felt I was the disturbing energy of resistance I talked about earlier. Then it's my own personal investigation. It's not like opening Ramana's book or Krishnamurti's book, and repeating the question, who am I? Who am I? Who am I?

The suffering and seeking brought me to the point where I felt I trusted what they were saying, but it wasn't my experience so I'm going to find out. The suffering brings you to the point where you look and say, what is this that I am? I felt this disturbing energy and I didn't like it. So what is this energy? And it's realized it's the sense of being in control, the sense of being a separate person. So is there any control? And it's just seen, no!

This separate entity I thought I was, this disturbing energy was based on a belief, and it's creating all of my suffering. So I look and see there's nothing here but a disturbing energy and a belief that I am in control, I am a separate, controlling entity.

So I question that and make it practical—can I control my experience? No! Thoughts arise. Feelings arise. Sensations arise. Actions happen. There's no one here! There's no one here controlling anything. So what am I? My entire life I thought I was this controlling entity. I am not that. So, what am I? I am this consciousness. And then there's a sense of relief, ahh. What a relief!

Now, it's like Stephen's life is on television. I can turn the television on and watch Stephen's life just happening. Either Stephen is a nice, kind, sweet guy or he's not. There's no separate entity here doing it. Whatever's happening is happening. Consciousness is watching.

I've always been this watching. There was no suffering when I was a child until this ego developed. From the time we're about two years old, and it gets bigger and bigger, stronger, heavier and more painful. This sense of ego, this sense of being separate is at the root of the suffering. We look and see there's nothing here. So there's a sense of relief as the resistance drops away. What's left? This witnessing, this watching that's always been here. It was here before the development of the ego in the human experience, it's here during the expression of the ego in the human experience, and it's here after—this witnessing.

That's why you'll hear this is not an attainment because you haven't *attained* this consciousness that you are. The peace we want is this consciousness that we are. Even as this activity and movement is happening here, my hands and arms are flailing about, I'm speaking loudly and I appear quite animated, consciousness is watching it! It doesn't matter what's happening here. I'm not doing it. There's no separate entity here. No one is doing anything. You think you're doing things! You're doing nothing! Everything is happening.

I don't care what your experience is. You think you're doing things, there's no one there doing anything! It's not possible for you to separate yourself from the rest of creation—Diana is over there and she can exercise control, it's not possible! Does an oak tree decide it's going to be an oak tree? And this year it decides it's not going to produce acorns and it wants to be a pine tree! That is absurd!

The capacity for thought has developed in the human experience, and the thought 'I' am in control arose in the human experience and it's believed. This is the fall from grace. Eating from the tree of the knowledge of good and evil—I know good from evil, I know right from wrong. It's the intellect, the mind.

The oak tree doesn't know good from evil—it just is. It is life itself and you are, too! But you have the capacity for thought. The thought 'I' arose and that's the birth of the appearance of separation. But there is no separation. Thought does not actually separate the universe into little pieces. The thought 'I' has no power!

Just because you think 'I am,' 'I am Diana' doesn't make it true! It's just a thought. The thought arises in the human experience, the thought 'I', and that is the birth of the appearance of separation, the fall from grace. Being separate from God, knowing good from evil you'll suffer all the days of your life—it's right in Genesis. If you believe 'I am Diana' you'll suffer. There's nothing you can do about it. That's the human experience. If 'I am Charles,' then Charles will suffer.

Charles: When you talk about separation, I get hung up on separation in form. I do see separation here in this room.

Stephen: No you don't.

Charles: [laughing in disbelief]

Stephen: It's a thought. Without thought there's no separation. Until thought arises, (you read J. Krishnamurti, right?)—you can see this in your own experience, until a thought arises there is no separation. If you don't have the thoughts, 'I am Charles, I see Stephen, I see the bottle,' there's no separation.

So, does thought actually separate the universe into little pieces or does it just appear so? It just appears so, because when there's no thought, there's no separation. If we remove one atom of hydrogen from the water molecules in your body, the whole thing falls apart. Nothing is separate. The air in this room goes into your body as you breathe it in, and then you exhale. The air in this room *is you*. The water in these bottles *is you*. There's no separation. Is the water in your body 'you', but the water in the bottle is *not you*? Are you only an atom of hydrogen? It's just a thought.

All of that is interesting talk. But at the root of psychological suffering is the birth of thought, 'I'. When the thought 'I' arises and the identification with this body and mind happens, that's the birth of the appearance of suffering—the fall from grace.

Charles: Can someone who has realized this continue to go about their daily life, or do they become a teacher or something? Because it seems if you think in terms of non-separation you couldn't go through your full day. I drive a delivery truck for a living, and I have to have a sense of separation to do that.

Stephen: Life is happening. Everything is already happening. You've never done anything. You're not doing anything now, and you were never doing anything. If you have the recognition that there is no Charles, Charles is just a concept—life is still happening. Your heart is beating right now—you're not beating your heart. Your eyes are seeing, Charles is not creating the seeing. Everything is happening, Charles has never done anything. The thoughts arose, 'I am Charles. I am the doer.' Those thoughts arose and are believed to be true. But even then, everything is simply happening.

The mysterious source, whatever it is that creates oak trees, dogs and cats, is creating every thought, feeling, sensation, and action in your experience. It's the same mysterious source. There's no separate Charles creating actions and there never was.

You posit that if someone has this recognition they wouldn't be able to go about their business—their business is already happening! It's already happening right now! Whatever it is that creates the oak tree is creating everything that's happening here. There's no separate entity creating anything. Could Charles separate himself from the mysterious source of all existence, God or Universal Intelligence, and then start doing his own thing? Is that possible? And if so, how did you do it? Having any sort of insight doesn't change what's happening. Universal life, this Mysterious Source is already expressing itself. It doesn't one day begin expressing itself after Charles realizes that Charles doesn't exist, and from that day, God takes control.

Lenny: But Lenny can choose...

Stephen: Choices happen. Lenny doesn't do anything! Lenny is an idea. Can an idea do anything? If you want another idea that's more accurate you could say Universal Intelligence makes choices—it's a mystery. Choices happen. Is there any individual chooser? If there is a separate chooser, Lenny, why would he ever choose sadness? Why wouldn't he choose happiness all the time? Could it be there is no separate Lenny there choosing? And the Mysterious Source is expressing itself? Could that be the case? If so, what is Lenny's role in

167

Lenny's life? He has no role!

The witnessing presence watches the show and you're done with trying to control. The uncomfortable sense of 'I want this, I don't want that' is based on a false belief in a separate Lenny. There's no one there. What's left for you to do? Nothing! Just watch. Everything is already being done!

The Mysterious Source of all existence, Intelligence Energy is already expressing itself! Every thought, feeling, sensation and action that's happening here is the same Mysterious Source expressing itself here, here, here, there [referring to everyone in the room] and through the oak tree. Even the sense of ego is an expression of the One Mysterious Source. There's nothing wrong with anything. Everything is what it is. If there's a sense of being separate, there's a sense of being separate. Did the ego create the ego? Everything is just happening.

Oh, wow! I get so fired up sometimes, Jason.

Jason: That's a good one—can the ego create the ego?

Lenny: But that's still a belief. Even this is still a belief.

Stephen: When you throw away all of your beliefs, what's left? What's left? Throw away all your beliefs, what's left?

Diana: Nothing. I want some water.

Stephen: Just this witnessing.

Lenny: I'm just playing.

Stephen: Me, too.

Jason: What was helpful for me was when you pointed out the 'seeing'. And the demonstration you did with seeing different objects, and noticing the 'seeing' is always the same. That really helped me. The seeing is always here, just the seeing. Sometimes finding the right word is helpful. It's this *seeing*. It's an action rather than an identity—it's just happening.

Stephen: Yes.

Jason: There's this seeing. That's what's happening—seeing. What I found is even when I'm at my most contracted, dense state, I see the contracted density perfectly—I don't like that state, and I see the disliking of it. When I'm happy, I see happiness with as much clarity as I see the contracted density.

Stephen: Yes.

Jason: The seeing is happening all the time.

Stephen: Yes, yes, that's it!

Jason: Regardless of what's being seen. I can't make the seeing stop. I don't remember making it begin.

Stephen: Right, yes.

Jason: It's always here.

Stephen: Yes, that's it.

Jason: The *seeing*, presence-awareness, or witnessing—it just happens.

Stephen: Yes, that's it.

Lenny: Is that a detachment from what is happening?

Stephen: No!

Jason: It's just happening. The seeing is impersonal. I'm not saying *Jason* is seeing. *The seeing is seeing Jason!* It's seeing everything.

Stephen: Yes.

Jason: It sees the good, it sees the bad.

Stephen: Yes. The seeing is neither detached, nor attached. It has nothing to do with any relative experience—it just *is*. It doesn't matter what is seen. Seeing is happening.

169

Diana: Anyway, I guess it's not helping me see right now, but it's okay. I don't have to see that.

Stephen: Okay, I have more to say, but I don't want you to yell at me.

[laughter]

Diana: Right, but somehow in this moment it's not helping me, and that's okay. Not everybody sees, and that's okay. Not everybody at all times has to see. Right now I don't see. I'm okay with that.

Jason: You're saying you don't see, but are you seeing that?

Diana: I'm seeing that I'm not seeing, and I'm okay with it.

Jason: But you're seeing it?

Stephen: Even seeing that you're not seeing is seeing.

Diana: I don't need to see that right now! It's okay. I'm okay with this tonight.

[laughter]

Stephen: Okay.

Diana: I don't have to see.

Jason: My point is that even when you see that you don't see something, you're still 'seeing'. The seeing is always here.

Diana: I don't know. Right now I don't need to see.

Jason: But you are seeing.

Diana: I just don't need to see!

Jason: But you are. You are seeing.

Diana: Well, that's what you're saying and telling me. But I'm okay with not seeing right now. I am at peace with it.

Jason: I think you are seeing.

[laughter]

Stephen: That's alright.

Diana: I'm okay with not seeing tonight.

[laughter]

Stephen: Yes, everything is okay.

Diana: Yes, thank you, very much.

Charles: When you said it was always here I remembered myself in front of my house when I was a child, and it does seem like it was the same seer. I wasn't any younger (the seeing).

Jason: Right. The intellect changes, and your body changes, and your emotions change, but I feel the same. I still feel like I did when I was four years old (the seeing) as I do now.

Charles: Yes.

Stephen: You remember yourself as a child walking to school. You recall this seeing was happening, and this is the same seeing now! It's seeing a different body, different experiences, different thoughts, different ideas, but the seeing is the same! So this is what's being pointed out, it's what I am. It doesn't change.
   It's the seeing, the consciousness, the awareness. You know it experientially so it doesn't matter which word we use. It's seeing different things. This is what we are—this consciousness. As we get older the seeing will be the same. We may end up in nursing homes, but the seeing will be the same!

Jason: The seeing doesn't age.

Stephen: It's timeless.

Jason: It's pure, clear consciousness.

171

Stephen: So this is what we are, we are eternal life, this witnessing presence—it's timeless.

Because the individual self, which is nothing but the mind, has lost the knowledge of its identity with the real Self, and has enmeshed itself in bondage, its search for the Self, its own eternal primal nature, resembles that of the shepherd searching for a lamb which all the time he bears on his shoulders. **—Ramana Maharshi**

36

The Mysterious Choiceless Awareness

Stephen: What's being pointed out is what you are in essence. It's the seeing. It doesn't change. The form will change and die. When this form dies, the life essence will express in a different form. So what am I? Am I this body or am I the life essence?

Jason: We also talked about the twilight state that's here upon waking up in the morning when you're coming to consciousness. It's a totally clear state. This happens to me when I've been in tremendous emotional turmoil. There's this twilight state and everything is peaceful. Then all of a sudden the 'I' thought comes in—boom, bang! And then the show starts. Where was the show ten seconds ago when I was in that peaceful state coming out of sleep? It's only upon awakening that the world comes in and the suffering begins. But even that is seen, just as the clarity is seen.

Stephen: Yes, you can notice the clear state when you wake up in the morning. There's a period of time before the mind starts, as Jason is saying. There's a period of peace prior to the mind thinking, 'I have to get up for work, I have to make breakfast,' ...I, I, I, I. Prior to the mind there's absolute awareness, and that is peace.

We notice there's no disturbance and there's no suffering until the 'I story' starts. And we notice it's only a story! *I am not in the story*, I am the *witnessing* of it. So I just watch and it does its thing. The body does its thing. The thoughts do their thing. All of that is watched— wow, look at that! Everything is happening. Consciousness is the same as when we were children. The body gets older, but it's the same *seeing*.

Charles: I heard Byron Katie say, no one wakes up in the morning and says, I think I'll think!

Stephen: Thinking happens.

Charles: Yes, that's when I really got the point that I don't have any control over thought at all.

Stephen: Thinking happens. It gets to the point where it doesn't matter what thoughts, feelings, or sensations are happening. So trying to control them stops. Trying to control them was the problem. We don't wake up in the morning and say, I think I'll think. We don't wake up and say, I think I'll feel. It just happens.

So there's a release and an acceptance of whatever is happening, because you have no choice—it's just happening anyway. This is surrendering to what *is*. There's a surrendering. It's not that 'I' surrender. It's not that I think I'll surrender now. This resistance falls away because it's seen the ego doesn't exist, it has no power. What do you do with a weapon that has no power? You toss it. It's useless. It has no power to control your experience.

Charles: There are a lot of traditions that say just the opposite. I went to an Evangelical Church; I went to my old Episcopal Church, I've been around—the whole approach is about control, and a lot of dogma.

Stephen: Yes. Certain points stand out in the different traditions. What stands out to me in the New Testament is some of the sayings of Jesus. When he says, "I can of my own self do nothing. I and the Father are One." Someone came to him and said, "Good Rabbi, how do we enter the Kingdom of Heaven?" He said, "Why do you call me good? There is one who is good, that is God. I can of my own self do nothing." Jesus is saying, "I can of my own self do nothing!" He's not doing anything. "I and the Father are One." I and Universal Life are One. So, where is this idea of control? Who's in control?

Charles: Yes, the mystical traditions talk about that.

Jason: The only thing that's always here is the seeing, the presence-awareness. It's undeniable. It's just here.

Stephen: Try to get out of it. Try not to see.

Jason: Try to get out of being aware.

Stephen: You can't do it.

Jason: What does Krishnamurti call it? It's choiceless awareness? There's no choice in it. It's just happening. And it is a mystery.

37

You and Me Are the Same Mystery

Darren: Do you get the sense that your awareness is the same as my awareness?

Stephen: It's a mystery. I have no idea what's happening here. This is a 'not knowing.' This is a mystery. These thoughts are happening, these eyes are seeing. There was the belief that I am seeing (me personally), I am looking out through these eyes. That belief drops and it's seen to be a mystery. How is all of this happening? See what I'm saying? So this is a mystery here. It's absolutely clueless.

This mystery is seen here. When I look at you I recognize the same mystery looking out of your eyes. I have no idea what's looking out of your eyes, and I have no idea what's looking out of my eyes. It's an absolute mystery how anything is happening. Before, there was the absolute conviction that Darren is in there and he's controlling actions and behaviors. So if Darren does anything bad to me, Darren is...

Darren: Responsible.

Stephen: Because there was a belief in a separate Stephen being here, that belief gets projected onto others.

Darren: Right.

Stephen: You notice when it drops *here* [referring to oneself] it immediately drops *there*—it's no longer projected. This mystery is here. We could say, now I'm projecting this *mystery* onto you. But that's all I know, this mystery.

Darren: That's very good. If I know that who is controlling the show *here* is not my mind, then I know that who is controlling the show *there* can't be anything else except...

Stephen: The same mystery.

Darren: Yes.

Stephen: So it's a mystery.

Darren: With you and me I can say this is my body, and that is your body. But with this mystery there is no 'my' mystery and 'your' mystery—it's just this *mystery*.

The arising of other gives rise to self;
giving rise to self generates others.
Know these seeming two as facets
of the One Fundamental Reality.
In this Emptiness, these two are really One
and each contains all phenomena.
—Seng-ts'an –Third Chinese Patriarch

The Mind is the Tool of Division

Stephen: There's no separation or psychological suffering in an oak tree, a flower or in dogs and cats because they don't have the capacity for thought. The human brain has developed so it has the capacity for thought. Thought is a tool. It's a tool we can use; it's a tool of division, separation, classification, and judgment. It's an effective tool for building bridges, building cars, and for science—all of that. It's an effective tool for manipulating the relative world. But it's not an effective tool to grasp the absolute. The mind, the human intellect is a tool for application in the relative world—use steel rather than plastic when building the Golden Gate Bridge. It compares and contrasts, divides, separates, and judges—this is better than that.

But for happiness, peace, love, and understanding the absolute, the mind can't do it because it's the tool of division. By definition the mind is a tool of division. It separates. So we're trying to use the mind to see that all is one. We're using the mind to find out if Darren's consciousness is the same as Stephen's. We can't use this tool because it's the tool of division. As soon as we say, 'my' consciousness and 'your' consciousness we've set up the appearance of separation. But there is no separation because thought doesn't actually separate anything. It's all one—whether we think it is or not. So we throw away this tool, and what's left is this consciousness—this solid block of reality.

It would be possible to describe everything scientifically, but it would make no sense; it would be without meaning, as if you described a Beethoven symphony as a variation of wave pressure.
—Albert Einstein

Free Will

Stephen: It's very simple to take apart the concept of free will and you'll see there is no free will. Not only is there no free will, there is no separate entity who can *exercise* free will. Whatever is expressing itself is a mystery. There are a lot of different words for it, Universal Intelligence, God, Life Itself, the Buddha Mind, Christ Consciousness, all these different terms.

Darren: So what do you do with your life?

Stephen: Life is happening. Everything is happening. It's like asking an oak tree that question. Just because there's a brain here doesn't mean it has any more control than an oak tree. What does an oak tree do with its life?

Darren: It just responds.

Stephen: It produces leaves and acorns. So what does this body do? Whatever the universe wants it to do. There's no way to know. We can ask, what is the purpose of the universe? Is there any way to know or is it a mystery? The purpose of the universe! If we have no idea what the purpose of the universe is, then how do we know the purpose of this tiny little speck in the universe? How would we know? How could we possibly know that?

Darren: Well, some people say it's easier to deal with one speck than the whole thing. But if the whole thing is meaningless, then the speck is meaningless also.

Stephen: I don't even know if it's meaningless. How could we say? Is there any way to know that? The entire universe!

Darren: Well, in the Landmark Forum they say your life is empty and meaningless. And it's empty and meaningless that it's empty and meaningless. So, don't make up some rationale as to why.

Stephen: Yes, I would say that's true. But I don't believe it because someone says it's true. That's what I see. I don't see how we could possibly know our purpose on a macro or absolute level.

Darren: So what does one do with one's life?

Stephen: One doesn't do anything. That's like asking an oak tree, what will you do with your life? There's no difference. What does an oak tree do with its life? It's an oak tree. What does a human being do with its life?—whatever the Universal Source does with it. It's like a puppet—no different than an oak tree.

Darren: I'm trying to see in practice how my stance would change if I realize I'm not in control. In the back of my mind I have the sense it's true. I did not choose to be in this seeker mode for the past thirty-five years. I did not want it. My best friend thinks the whole thing is nonsense, and he has a great life. I didn't choose this. My head went into the tiger's mouth, and I got stuck. That tells me I had no say in the matter. I have some sense it's true. My question is if I were to shift my perspective to seeing I'm not the one in control, what next? What next?

Stephen: What's next is just watching. If you are not the one in control, then what are you? A thought comes in, a feeling, a sensation, and then an action happens. Everything is happening spontaneously. There's nothing that is *not* spontaneous.

So we see there is no individual free will. I'm not a controlling entity. I am consciousness. What is the role of consciousness? It just watches, it witnesses. So, what do I do? I watch. I witness. I watch the activities of the body/mind.

Darren: You mean the big 'I', not the ego. The 'I' that runs the show.

Stephen: Yes, there's just one I. It's what you are—this life essence that's aware of everything. You ask, what happens when you realize this—*you watch.* There's nothing else to do, because everything is being done.

The Way is always uncontrived, yet there's nothing it doesn't do.
—Tao Te Ching

40

Do You Know Anything at All?

Darren: Let me ask you this: even the mind we have, use and need was put here by this Mystery, right?

Stephen: It's just happening. That's a concept—this Mystery. When I try to understand what's happening here, what's seeing everything in the room here, and what perceives this? It's a mystery. That's why I say, this Mysterious Source. Then we observe everything in the appearance and say, that's the Mysterious Source expressing itself. I find no separation between the Mysterious Source, what I am, what you are, and everything is. It's all One. *I am* the Mysterious Source. *You are* the Mysterious Source.

Darren: It's all the Mysterious Source.

Stephen: It's all the Mysterious Source. It's one solid block of reality—one solid block of God.

Darren: I now realize my struggle to make sense of all this is perhaps what I must let go of. Because I'm trying to make sense of something that cannot be understood. When you keep using the word *mystery*, I think that's my salvation—to embrace that it's a mystery.

Stephen: Yes, burn out the intellect. You try so hard it implodes on itself. There's no way to know anything absolutely. There's no way to know anything absolutely because all knowledge is relative. What is it relative to? When you say, 'I know this,' it's relative to something. When you notice the foundation upon which all knowledge is built is a fabrication—there's no way to know anything.

Darren: And, hence, whatever you build onto this fabrication is all...

Stephen: It all falls apart. What's left is this witnessing that's happening. And I know nothing. So this is a *not* knowing. Advaita is *not* two. When you see that you know nothing and there is not two—that's it. There's nothing.

Darren: That's the end of the quest.

Stephen: That's it. I Am. There's no separate self to realize. There's nothing to do, nowhere to go—that's it!

When you say, "I really don't know," what happens? The mind becomes completely humble. Now that state of 'not knowing' is intelligence.
                                                      —**J. Krishnamurti**

Part II Correspondence

1

I Thought, 'How Obvious—Damn!'

Chet: The day before yesterday I was depressed from thoughts about not understanding. Reading wasn't helping—nothing was helping.

I came across your email below from our correspondence several months ago. When I read what is highlighted, and the words "This awareness is your essential nature," a flash of light literally went off in my head, and I thought how obvious—damn! It *is* simple, and I have noticed the nature of the illusory 'I'.

> "Words imply a duality where none exists. It's the nature of language, but we don't need words to know this presence of awareness that we are. Now, I'm using words and I'm asking if you can stop for a moment, right now, and notice the fact that you are aware of these words. More accurately, there is awareness of these words, right?
>
> If we drop the words, drop the language, and sense for ourselves what the words are pointing to, we are aware, and we know it. Something is witnessing these words, something is aware of the room in which you're sitting, something is aware of the sounds you're hearing in the background, something is aware of the thoughts that are arising in response to the words you're reading now. So, there is awareness here, yes?
>
> This awareness is your essential nature, my essential nature. Without this awareness, nothing exists. The thought, 'be aware of awareness,' does not exist unless awareness is here to witness it. The phrase, 'be aware of awareness,' is just a pointer to help bring attention away from the objects of awareness and back to awareness itself."

I've read a lot of authors and you lit up my life. Thanks so much.

Stephen: Thank you for writing. Yes, it is obvious, aye?

I Got Back Into Seeking Again

Mary: Well, here's my latest report. I got all convoluted back into seeking and ended up getting involved in another spiritual movement. Anyway, who knows what that movement is for all concerned, but for me, now it's bye-bye to the future and anything that's going to happen later. I just looked at an email from you I had saved, and I got trapped in the same way you did:

> "Initially the suffering returned for me because I somehow had the false expectation that I should have had the 'ultimate' shift, I should have no negative emotions, I should never drink alcohol, I should never feel anger, etc. See how the same old beliefs come back in? The I shoulds and I shouldn'ts? There are *no* shoulds and shouldn'ts. *Everything* is free to come and go through us. We didn't create anything that arises in awareness and we can't control what comes and goes."

So true! Now I'm not waiting for some ultimate shift. What a relief to stop thinking something special has to happen. THIS is it. Just *be here*. Thanks for your help along the way! Freedom is freedom to be every experience.

If doubt comes back in it's just a thought coming into this present awareness. No more or less important than that. Why make it important? Habit I guess—back to presence.

Stephen: Yes, it seems our spiritual path can be either a playground or a battleground. When we see we are already free, and we're already the One, we are free to enjoy and play with our spiritual interests on the playground of life.

But when we're seeking, hoping, and striving to attain something better or different than what we already are, our spiritual path becomes a battleground. And there's no peace or love on a battleground.

You have always been one with the Buddha, so do not pretend you can attain this Oneness by various practices. —**Zen Master Huang Po**

Your Spiritual Search is a Joke

Daniel: I feel I'm finally ready to let the I-concept go, but something is keeping me from making the final step. I have been a seeker for many years, but I'm ready for it to end. Any advice or help would be greatly appreciated.

Stephen: If you're ready to let go of the I-concept, then hang on to it as long as you can. Don't let go. If the I-concept fades, try to get it back. If you get it back, try to let it go again.

What comes and goes cannot be you. You are always here watching what comes and goes. There's nothing that needs to be let go of. There's nothing that needs to be held on to.

Your spiritual search is a joke. You will never attain freedom from the I-concept. You will never attain enlightenment. You are the 'watching' so just watch.

Daniel: Thanks for your response. I was somewhat surprised to hear you say that my spiritual search is a joke, and I would never attain freedom from the I-concept or enlightenment either, for that matter.

After reflecting on your comments, however, I agree completely. Searching is a joke, as Ramana said, since that which you are searching for is that which you already are. Also, freedom and enlightenment cannot be obtained since they, too, already are. I am, however, ready to stop seeking.

Stephen: Yes, you are what you're seeking. So what are you? Stop and notice it now. Stop and notice that you are that which is seeing these words. Stop, right now, and notice in your own direct experience that what you are is this 'seeing'.

You are that which is watching Daniel and his spiritual search. You are that which is aware of the I-concept, and aware of the desire to be free of the I-concept. You are that which is already free.

This 'seeing' that you are, this watching, this awareness is unaffected by Daniel's spiritual search, untouched by the I-concept. This 'seeing' that you are is already here. This awareness that you are need not be sought. So what do you need to do to be free of the seeking and the I-concept? Notice that you are already free. Notice it now.

4

Points of Consciousness in Awareness

Cliff: There is one question that's been bothering me for a long time. I know I am awareness, but I can't understand how there can be only *one* awareness. Your story is being experienced by awareness and so is my story. Yet, I'm not aware of your story, and you are not aware of mine. How can that be if we are the same awareness? If I am the One awareness, shouldn't I experience all people's minds, the whole universe, and everything in it right now?

Stephen: You have one body with two hands. If you hit your left hand with a hammer, your left hand will hurt, but not your right hand. You have one body that has many points of consciousness.

There is one body of awareness that is the universe. This One body of awareness has many points of consciousness. Cliff is conscious of his story, but not Stephen's. There is One body of awareness with many points of consciousness.

Is your left hand separate from your right hand, or are they of One body? Is Cliff's story separate from Stephen's story, or are they of the One body of Awareness?

Cliff: You mean everything is living in the one awareness: all the stars, people, you, me, animals, every cell, every atom. And all these things, cells, people etc. are just separate points of consciousness in the one awareness?

Are there billions of stories going on right now in awareness, but Cliff can't see it since he has a consciousness that is separated from the other consciousnesses in the one awareness?

Stephen: Prior to the I-thought, *all is.* As soon as the I-thought arises, the appearance of separation arises. That's why you (Cliff, I) are frustrated trying to know that all is One. Cliff, as the thought 'I' cannot know Oneness, because the I-thought has already created the appearance of separation. So 'I', which is the birth of the appearance of duality, am trying to know Oneness which is the absence of 'I'.

Be still and know that I AM God.

Cliff: Do you know a good book that talks about this—how we are different points of consciousness in awareness?

Stephen: From Nisargadatta's *I AM THAT*: "You are and I am. But only as points in consciousness; we are nothing apart from consciousness."

Awareness comes first. A bundle of memories and mental habits attracts attention, awareness gets focalized and a person suddenly appears. Remove the light of awareness, go to sleep or swoon away, and the person disappears. The person flickers, awareness contains all space and time—the absolute is.

—**Nisargadatta Maharaj**

186

The Guy Who Thought it Was All Done

Vinci: As usual, I'm back to not understanding squat again! I'm really stuck on the body, and this sense that awareness is localized in the body. I seem to be okay for a while, and then back I go to the difficulties. Sometimes I feel this will never be over for me. Any chance you would be willing to talk again? The guy who thought it was all done and then...

Stephen: "Awareness is localized in the body. Awareness is localized in the refrigerator. Awareness is localized in the phone book."
    All thoughts arising in awareness.

"I finally have this understanding. I lost this understanding. I don't understand this understanding."
    All thoughts arising in awareness.

"I had it and then I lost it. I lost it and then I got it back again. I never had it. I never lost it."
    All thoughts arising in awareness.

"The body is the source of awareness. Awareness is the source of the body. The brain is the source of awareness. I am the body. I am the brain. I am a dog. I am awareness."
    All thoughts arising in awareness.

You are the *nothing* that everything appears in. You are nothing and everything. You cannot be lost or attained. It's not possible.

Behold an emblem of our human mind
Crowded with thoughts that need a settled home
Yet, like to eddying balls of foam
Within this whirlpool, they each other chase
Round and round, and neither find
An outlet nor a resting-place!
—William Wordsworth

How Can You Say, 'All is One?'

Jeremy: Right now there is a deeper understanding that the being-ness without any 'my' to it is underlying, embracing, and enfolding all of this. The persistence of memories, images, voices, logical arguments, etc. are being witnessed as changeable phenomena.

Stephen: Yes, you are the consciousness, the witnessing, the seeing of the changeable phenomena. Without your presence as consciousness, there can be no phenomena. This consciousness that you are is the essential prerequisite of all phenomena. Notice that consciousness is witnessing these words right now. Without consciousness being here now, these words do not exist. These words have no independent existence. Without consciousness, nothing exists.

Jeremy: There is a strong thought, almost like a rip tide, that is persistent. In fact it is a question: how can this sense of being be described as 'all there is' or as universal, that is, something that everyone or everything has?

Stephen: Consciousness is not something that everyone or everything *has*. Consciousness is what everyone and everything *is*. Life is not something that everyone or everything *has*. Life is what everyone and everything *is*.

Consciousness is the essence of all existence, all phenomena. Can anything exist if consciousness is not here to witness it? Does the universe exist if consciousness is not here to witness it? Does anything exist outside or separate from consciousness? What are you in essence? What are other people in essence? What are dogs and cats in essence? What are birds, flowers, and trees in essence? What is the universe in essence? What is life? Are you separate from the universe? Are you separate from life? Is anything separate from the universe? Is anything separate from life?

Consciousness is life itself. The universe is life itself. The universe is alive. And you are that life. You cannot possibly be separate from universal life itself.

When does the appearance of separation begin? Does the appearance of separation begin with thought? Does thought actually divide the universe into separate entities or does it just appear so? Can any thought be witnessed without consciousness being here to witness it?

Is consciousness separate? Is 'your' consciousness separate from 'my' consciousness? When does consciousness become separate? Is it when the thoughts 'I, me or mine' arise? Does the thought 'mine' actually divide consciousness or does it just appear so? Can the thought 'mine' exist if consciousness is not here to witness it? Who is this 'me' that says 'mine'? Is this 'me' just a thought? Does the thought 'me' have any separate existence from consciousness? Is the thought 'me' alive or conscious?

Jeremy: As this question arises, there is an equally persistent determination which recognizes even that question is another 'yes, but,' and any thought whatsoever is only trying to divide. But the doubt does linger.

Stephen: Yes, thought is the appearance of division, the appearance of separation. But upon investigation it's noticed that thought has no independent, separate existence. The thoughts 'I, me, and mine' appear to divide life into separate entities—me-you, us-them, God-human, spirit-matter. There is no real separation, only conceptual, thought-based, imaginary.

If thought does not actually divide the universe into separate entities, then separation never happened. All is One—or not two.

There is one universe. There is one life. This life is all there is, and you are that. There is one consciousness. Consciousness is all there is, and you are that. All is One. You are that One, I am that One, All is that One. There is no separation.

Jeremy: I clearly see the transient nature of everything that is going on in this present moment. It really can't have a center. There have been moments of total quiet in the mind recently, and moments of loudness and ferocity. Some of the static is 'I don't get it' or 'why did I freak out' or 'how will my conversation with the landlord go' etcetera. Even though it's clear there is no one asking these questions. But the questions are unpleasant.

Right now all I know for sure is this completely untouchable, seemingly empty existence—the being. I can feel it. It's quite literally a no-brainer. I don't know what life is. I don't know what non-duality is. I don't know what the universe or consciousness is, or death, or

189

what 'everything' or 'nothing' means. I can't grasp that really—it has no substance for me.

All I know is that when thoughts are left alone there is peace. Then there's the thought that '*not* understanding' is somehow giving up, and I need to feel life is all of this and I am life or consciousness or the universe. Followed by another thought that I just have to throw it all out and let the train move on.

In writing this I see it can go on forever, enumerating the thoughts. But I think it's helpful to see these thoughts. At this point these thoughts seem to be really strong habits.

If you attach even to a trace
of this and that, of right and wrong,
the Mind-essence will be lost in confusion.
Although all dualities arise from the One,
do not be attached even to ideas of this One.
—Seng-ts'an –Third Chinese Patriarch

7

These Words Apply to *You*

Vinci: I thought I'd write to let you know where I am currently with this stuff. I want to stick to what I know as opposed to ideas about it. I thought the best way to do that might be in an email to you so you could let me know if you think I'm off base or on target.

Right now, there is awareness of typing happening. There is awareness of sensations in the hands and fingers and rear end on the chair! There is awareness of thinking—including these very thoughts that are appearing on this screen. There is awareness of a thought 'I am typing' as well as the thought 'there is no I.' Both are thoughts occurring within awareness.

There is no one here who planned to type this thought. The thought occurred and typing happened. Then there is the thought 'what do you mean, of course I'm thinking and typing'—and there is awareness of that thought arising and now it is gone and replaced by these very words being typed and read right now.

This is all happening immediately—this moment, now this moment, now this moment. No independent 'doer' is found. All these objects arise but no one who is doing them, and they arise to this awareness.

Am I this body/brain? Well, all that can be said on direct looking and direct experience is that body parts are seen, and sensations felt, and thoughts observed. This can be seen directly. The thought 'I am this body/brain' is just that—a thought arising within and as awareness.

No independent decision-maker or self-powered 'I' can be found outside of thought. As Bob Adamson says, this brain is simply a transformer for the Intelligence-Energy—the thoughts that arise are after the fact of this Livingness that we are. In fact, to say 'livingness' and 'we' is really too much—it's all just Livingness.

Will I die? Yes and no. This body will likely go the way of all other forms—it will disintegrate in some fashion and stop functioning in its current manner. Will this Livingness die? Hmm. It appears that so-called death will happen within this awareness. Death is another arising to this unchanging awareness that is the obvious and testable background on which these thoughts—including 'death' thoughts—are occurring. But the observable fact is that all of this is more thinking and conceptualizing arising right now on and as this Livingness.

Will I become enlightened? No. The 'I' is a thought. Thoughts just arise and pass away within this awareness. Thoughts don't become enlightened. There really is no one to become enlightened. All that arises, whether stories about enlightenment or un-enlightenment, is imagination. These same stories are seen by and known by this awareness. 'Working towards' enlightenment or 'giving up the search' are still both arising within awareness—THIS.

Do I finally get it? No. The I-thought will never get it. It can't—it's a thought. But, at least there is awareness of it as a thought rather than as a reference to something real. So there is no one to get it. There is just awareness of these thoughts arising now—that's all that can ever be. Thinking there can be awareness of something tomorrow is just that—thoughts arising right now to no one.

And there really isn't anything to get. It's just seeing 'what is' rather than taking what arises to be what is real and permanent. Whatever arises, arises. There is no one and nothing to be done about it. It is all free to come and go—including the thought 'I don't want it to come and go.'

I've kept this as close to the bone as I can right now, not wanting to fly off into conceptualization—a land in which I have found absolutely no satisfaction. My new definition of suffering, by the way, is the spiritual search itself!

Stephen: Yes, what's being pointed to is the watching, the seeing, the witnessing of all that arises. What's being pointed out is that you are the consciousness in which everything arises.

The objects that arise in you are not given any relevance in this teaching. The objects are thoughts, feelings, sensations, images, stories, dramas, fears, memories, and projections. The questions of how, why, when, what if, yes but, are objects arising in you, consciousness. The objects of consciousness are always changing—you remain as the witnessing presence of all that arises.

You are the witnessing presence. Notice it now. Knowing yourself as the witnessing presence of all that arises is the resolution of all spiritual seeking, and psychological suffering.

Everything is free to come and go through you, and you remain untouched, peaceful and free. Getting involved in the questions, stories and dramas, and trying to figure it all out, and get it all right is the very suffering you're trying to overcome. Nothing can trouble you but imagination. Knowing yourself as this simple witnessing presence is the resolution to all your seeking and suffering. It *is* this simple, and you know it.

Vinci: Here is something I saw yesterday really clearly—what I refer to as 'I' really is a thought—it's the thought 'I'. Here's what I mean: there was a lot of thinking floating around about Advaita, getting it, not getting it, etc. and the thought arose, 'I really don't get it.' Something happened and it occurred to me to ask 'What or where is this 'I' that doesn't get it?' It became really clear that this 'I' was literally a thought that arose again and again and that all kinds of other thoughts attached to it. For just a moment, thinking ground to a halt. It seems very clear there really is NO ONE to 'get it.' It's all just thinking arising and passing away about getting it or not getting it and on and on and on—and I am not thinking, i.e. there is no one here deciding what to think or not to think. Even right now, I am not deciding what to write—thoughts just occur and writing happens—weird.

Another revelation: I heard and read about teachers (it might have been Ramana originally) who said, if you paid attention, you could see the 'I' arise after waking in the morning. I was looking for something kind of mystical or other worldly to happen and I never saw it happen. Then, yesterday morning, I saw the I-thought arise—nothing stupendous or earth-shattering. I just saw the first 'I' come up whereas before it arose, there was just moving around, turning off the alarm, etcetera. And I get it that 'I' don't see anything—it is all just arising within awareness.

Let me ask, for you, has thinking just stopped arising for the most part? Or is there little or no interest in the thinking that arises (other than the practical thinking that might have to do with simple functioning—obviously that is arising). It probably doesn't matter, does it? The deal is seeing/relaxing into the background that I am, we are, because moving into the conceptual world is where the problems occur, isn't it?

Stephen: All thoughts, feelings, and sensations are free to come and go through you. You are that which is aware of thoughts, feelings, and sensations. You are awareness itself. Thoughts, feelings, and sensations arise on their own and are witnessed. Notice you are the witnessing presence. Notice there is no separate person called Vinci who is creating the thoughts, feelings, and sensations—there is only consciousness. Vinci is an appearance in you. Vinci does not exist unless you are there to witness him. Vinci has no power to create or avoid any thoughts, feelings, or sensations that appear. Vinci is just another appearance in you, consciousness.

You've seen in your own direct experience that you, consciousness, are there before Vinci appears and before the thought 'I' appears. You are that which witnesses the appearance of Vinci and the thought 'I'. Knowing yourself as this simple witnessing presence that is always here, even now, is the resolution of all spiritual seeking, and psychological suffering.

You are the nothing that all thoughts, feelings, and sensations arise in. You are timeless, spaceless, shapeless, and formless. You are the emptiness and the timeless-ness in which all space and time appear. These words apply to you. These words describe what you are in essence. You have always been this simple witnessing presence. *You* are the resolution to all seeking and suffering.

EVERYTHING is free to come and go through you. You remain untouched, peaceful and free.

Oh Companion That Abode Is Unmatched,
Where My Complete Beloved Is.

In that Place There Is No Happiness or Unhappiness,
No Truth or Untruth
Neither Sin nor Virtue.
There Is No Day or Night, No Moon or Sun,
There Is Radiance Without Light.

There Is No Knowledge or Meditation
No Repetition of Mantra or Austerities,
Neither Speech Coming from Vedas or Books.
Doing, Not-Doing, Holding, Leaving
All These Are Lost Too In This Place
—Kabir

What Does Nisargadatta Mean By This?

Cliff: I read on your website a quote by Nisargadatta. I don't understand what he means. Do you think you could help me understand this text? I'd appreciate it a lot. Here's the quote:

> "There is absolutely no difference between me and others, except in my knowing myself as I am. I know it for certain, and you do not. The difference is only in the mind and temporary. I was like you, you will be like me."

Stephen: What is your interpretation of that quote?

Cliff: When Nisargadatta says, "There is absolutely no difference between me and others, except in my knowing myself as I am. I know it for certain and you do not."

I see it like this: there is no difference between any people except that I know Cliff's story, and Nisargadatta knows Nisargadatta's story.

Nisargadatta says: "The difference is only in the mind and temporary. I was like you, you will be like me."

I see it like this: when Cliff dies he will be reborn as Nisargadatta and Nisargadatta will be reborn like Cliff.

Stephen: Wow, that's quite a story! But, I don't see any reference to being re-born—either stated or implied. That's not my interpretation.

Cliff: As I think about this a bit more—maybe he meant: there is no difference between us since we are all the same One, the same self. The difference is Nisargadatta knows himself as the source, whereas most people take themselves to be separate. The difference is only in most people's minds.

Nisargadatta means he was like most people, taking himself as a separate individual, but sees himself as the source now. And in time, other people will see themselves as the source, too, just like Nisargadatta does. Maybe this was what he meant. Is this it? Is this what he meant?

Stephen: Yes, that's my interpretation of what he meant.

Enlightenment is the Problem Not the Solution

David: I sent an email to you a few months ago regarding non-duality. But, no matter what, I still can't see this. It seems very obvious right now that all there is, is awareness, and this is all there ever has been. Any thought of a person has been just that, a thought, and not a reality. However, in seeing this, there are no feelings of peace, and during everyday life the story continues, and so does the suffering.

I understand there is nothing to find so why is there a distinction between those who get this and those who don't? It seems when the mind sees itself as false, the story is automatically dropped (like the analogy of the snake being a rope). But no matter how many times it is seen that awareness is all there is, the story continues.

Stephen: What is your experience when you are suffering? Exactly what is happening? I can't find any entity here who is suffering, can you find one there? I find a series of stories revolving around an imaginary character called Stephen. I find no one real who is suffering. I find nothing but imaginary characters and an imaginary story of suffering. I find no real suffering or no real character who suffers. I believed I was suffering for twenty-five years, but I looked into this Stephen character, and I looked into what I was calling suffering, and I found nothing but imagination. What do you find?

David: I understand there is no one here just this presence of awareness, however, even though there is no real central character to these stories, when they come up, the body responds creating physical pain and resistance. I have looked countless times and see nothing but this consciousness with a lot of pain in it which takes the joy out of life. Maybe I am only seeing this on the surface level and it needs to be seen on a deeper level that there is only consciousness?

Stephen: Suffering is all imaginary, isn't it? If there is no story playing in your head, can there be any suffering? You don't have to (nor can you) get rid of the stories that are playing in your head. You just notice all the stories are imaginary, and all suffering is based on the imaginary character, David, who is the star of the stories.

There is no such thing as suffering, no one who can suffer. There's no such thing as enlightenment and no one who can be enlightened. It's all imagination. There's nothing deeper than that.

Are you really suffering, or is that, too, a story playing of David, the poor, suffering man? And someday David will be enlightened! It really is this simple—just seeing David and his suffering are imaginary. Then if the stories continue to play in the head, to whom does it matter? Just watch the stories—so what!

David: I understand that suffering is imaginary, but knowing it conceptually isn't enough. I feel I am missing something, or I have not seen this in the right way. People who get this seem to immediately become very peaceful and talk about having a sense that everything is one. And they are able to preach this to other people from first hand experience, where I would have to refer to other's texts to explain this to people. Am I reading too deep into this, or is there some final understanding?

Stephen: Well, either suffering is imaginary or it's not. Is your suffering imaginary? Don't agree conceptually—consider your own experience. Is there any suffering for you when there is no imaginary story playing in your head? Seeing that for yourself is not a conceptual understanding—it's an experiential or non-conceptual recognition that nothing can trouble you but imagination.

In your own direct experience you see that if you feel you are suffering, then you know there's a story playing about David—David is not good enough, David doesn't get it, David is... you know the story!

All the talk you're hearing from other people is part of the story that's playing in your head. Other people get this, and I don't. Other people know all is one and are free of suffering, and I am not. What's wrong with me?

Look in your own experience. Is suffering imaginary? What am I in essence? Can I really suffer, or is that an imaginary story playing in my head? What am I really? Am I this simple consciousness that is watching these stories play before me? Am I David or is David a character in the play I'm watching?

Trying to improve David and his experience, trying to free David of his suffering, trying to make David become enlightened, peaceful and free, hoping to get what others seemingly have—all of that is the problem. There is no real problem other than the solution! The solution implies a problem that doesn't exist, and someone who can attain the resolution to suffering, enlightenment or some other conceptual nonsense.

All there is—check this for yourself—is this consciousness right now, right now, right now. Everything else is imagination. See if that's true—don't accept it or reject it. It is this simple.

[Follow up a few days later]

David: Today there was a seeing for the first time that consciousness is all there is! Everything was so hilarious—the searching, the belief there was a separate person—what a joke! It was only a temporary seeing, however, now it is known that even though the feeling of being an individual may come back, there is only ever consciousness! Thank you for helping me see this.

I am always with all beings
I abandon no one.
However great your inner darkness
You are never separate from me.

Let your thoughts flow past you calmly
Keep me near at every moment
Trust me with your life, because I
Am you, more than you yourself are.
—Bhagavad Gita

10

I Expected More, Bigger and Better

Cameron: I stumbled onto your website recently and found the words on your web page to be potent. Something settled in and I had a very basic clarity about the whole business. You see, I have touched this basic peace before, and found it to be very satisfying and full, yet I expected there to be more or bigger or better, so I keep going from book to book, teaching to teaching.

Now I am full of questions and ideas about it, and some doubts. I would like to enquire about a telephone consultation with you, as your way of putting it seems to have a big impact on me.

[After a telephone conversation, the emails below followed]

Cameron: I have a few more questions. Ever since our last talk there has been this total ease of being, nothing seemed to be much of a problem. Even, I guess, things that objectively would be rated as problems were just happening, and they all just do their thing and passed—so simple! There are no real problems it seems.

Yet about a day ago the 'I' sense started arising quite strongly and the problems seemed to be more real, very convincing. But I stayed with the pith instruction, 'Just watch'—so there was suffering and I watched. Then inexplicably today it was gone again and that ease of being is back.

So, I am a bit confused. Although the suffering was taking center stage for a day, when I look at it today it seems so silly—just a story. It also seemed to be a very real happening. I could see and clearly feel that peace of basic awareness, yet it seemed pushed back by the story. So there was a continuum of watching, and in that sense this vivid ease and peace was there too, very dimly in the background, but now it is primary again.

Is this how it works? Suffering and the I-sense every so often arise strongly again, I simply watch, and then it subsides and reverts back to the natural state?

Stephen: The experience you've described is quite common. There has been a belief in the stories for many years. Now you know the stories and the central character in the story, Cameron or 'I', are not true. You know you are the witnessing presence of all the stories, so you just watch.

So why do the stories and the central character, Cameron, take center stage and appear to disturb the peace at times? Well, the stories have been playing for many years, and there was a belief that the stories were true, and a belief that you were Cameron, the central character. Habit is a function of the mind, so the stories may come up at times and appear to disturb the peace. What do you do? You watch. That's it.

Do you see that if there is any attempt to change or avoid the stories that are playing it's more of the same egoic desire to control? Any attempt to alter or avoid the stories is more of the same old egoic involvement and suffering.

But if you simply watch the stories that play out in the head, you'll notice a new perspective, and a new habit forming in your experience. Knowing yourself as the witnessing presence of all that's happening becomes your daily experience—it is your natural state.

There is nothing to do to make this happen—consciousness is already your natural state—you just watch and let the stories play out. You'll notice the stories become more entertaining, and less troublesome. The stories are quite entertaining—so you watch them!

Cameron, you have a solid understanding and direct experience of this. Everything is working itself out nicely.

The arising and the elimination of illusion are both illusory. Illusion is not something rooted in Reality; it exists because of dualistic thinking. If you will only cease to indulge in opposed concepts such as 'ordinary' and 'Enlightened', illusion will cease of itself.
—**Zen Master Huang Po**

11

Not Just a Cute Spiritual Metaphor

Cameron: I thought I should keep in touch and let you know how things have been unfolding (seemingly) for me. The past two weeks were tremendously euphoric (as I'm sure you noticed in my last correspondence). Basically the very blissful bodily experience, of course, subsided. Once it left there was some anxiety and scrambling to get it back and to try to 'do' what I did before, which is obviously a mistaken presumption based on the notion that there was someone who had done something before! Anyway, after much frustration and then a somewhat melodramatic giving up moment, everything settled down nicely and now there is just this very simple, ordinary way of being—just as I am always.

It has been interesting to watch this because there really was this belief that there was someone who needed to do something, you know, to sustain or continue it or something. So it's been interesting to see I can actually forget about the understanding altogether—and everything still is just fine as it is. There is no need to actively think about it or anything, which as I write this I know sounds silly—but that is the classic me story "gotta be non-dual today! I am non-dual Cameron after all," but that's all rubbish.

It just is everything. And sometimes during the day something will happen or someone will say something and it will just pop into my head "Oh! She thinks she is someone." Or weirder stuff like the other day it dawned on me there is no difference between animate and inanimate objects—these are just words that make my is-ness seem different, for example, to a rock or a tree.

And of course this really means there can be no death, or life for that matter—it's all this fluid sameness. Oh, yeah, and my favorite one—I used to think that 'now' was this spot where I was that somehow moved along the timeline, but its so obvious that it's all now. I know it's been said in all the books and everything. But it's so, well, literal. Just now, that's all there ever was. It's almost silly to call it 'now' because it has nothing to do with time and what people perceive as time is just this bubbling of energy called trees, and rocks and Cameron right here out of this supposed 'now'. Well, I guess I am preaching to the choir here but its fun to write about it anyway.

One question though: 'Just watch'—does this require effort? Or is 'Just watch' what we are already are, and hence it requires no effort?

Stephen: You may notice there is no such thing as effort. And there is no separate person who exerts effort. Thoughts happen and sometimes actions follow: Whose thoughts are they? Whose effort is it? Is there any separate entity there who has thoughts, and exerts effort?

Does a pine tree make an effort to produce pine cones? Does a dog make an effort to bark? Does the wind make an effort to blow? You are awareness. Is there any effort required to be awareness, or is awareness simply happening?

The suggestion to 'just watch' is given to act as a pacifier for a busy mind that wants to know, "What do I do? What happened to my bliss? How can I get it back? How can I avoid these disturbing thoughts?" The answer is nothing needs to be done. Bliss happens. Disturbing thoughts happen. Peace happens.

Believing there is a separate entity who needs to do something about his experience, and trying to change the experience is at the root of suffering.

The suggestion to 'just watch' acts as a pacifier to the mind, and takes you out of the story of a suffering 'me' and helps you notice that you are the awareness that is watching the show—not the imaginary, suffering 'me'.

Cameron: In order to resolve some of my final doubts I have been spending the last two days trying to articulate to myself how I understand things—in the most reduced, pithy way, in order to pinpoint where these doubts are coming from. This is where I am—perhaps by explicating it like this you can point out the doubt's source: It's undeniably clear to me that what we are is this uncaused peace, and this is our empty awareness. This is always available in the sense that we are it, yet suffering happens when we believe that instead of this knowing nothingness, we are a fixed person. So when I reduce it on a tangible level it's about an uncaused peace which is indestructible and untouchable by changing conditions whether they are external or imaginary. When I am confident that I am this uncaused peace, nothing that the character does or says, or anything that happens to that character is such a big deal anymore because fundamentally this peace is certain one-hundred percent.

On the other hand there is psychological suffering which comes down to believing that, instead of peace being the essential, irrevocable

202

aspect of your own being, you are a separate thing that must go out and find peace in other separate things 'out there'—from this point of view peace is not what you *are* but something that you can get and lose, based on circumstances.

So, it seems to me the possibility of suffering comes in when the 'I' sense arises strongly enough to make you believe that, indeed, the peace you are is *out there* and has been tampered with—to make you believe you have lost it somehow.

My doubt is this: It seems to me that because you have no control over what happens, including the arising of the 'I' sense, your peace is contingent on whether or not the 'I' arises. This makes me question whether I have seen through it completely. Because although I feel a deep conviction that there is no one at all, and I feel entirely at ease at this moment, there is this nagging threat the habitual patterning of the 'I' sense will arise and then no amount of non-dual understanding will change the fact that I am suffering based on that 'I' arising strongly enough to make me think the story is true.

It seems to me you are either buying the illusion or seeing the truth. And if there is the possibility of suffering, for whatever reason (other than basic physical pain), the 'I' is still lingering, then the truth has not been seen fully.

Stephen: In your own direct experience, what's happening when psychological suffering is happening? Isn't thinking happening? Thinking about Cameron? Usually a story is playing in the head, and, of course, the central character in the story is Cameron.

Is there *ever* any psychological suffering when there is no story playing? Of course not! If there is no story playing in the head, there is no psychological suffering. Another name for the stories playing in the head is imagination. So, isn't it clear that all psychological suffering is based on imagination?

Sometimes the imaginary stories create an uncomfortable energy in the body, and we call this process psychological suffering. So psychological suffering is nothing more than imagination and an uncomfortable energy in the body. What do you do when disturbing stories are playing and uncomfortable energy is flowing through the body? You watch. Nothing needs to be done.

You are the witnessing presence. You witness the pleasant stories and the unpleasant. You witness the pleasurable sensations and the unpleasant. You may notice there really is no such thing as psychological suffering. To say you are suffering psychologically is just another story playing and you watch it.

You are the witnessing presence that is aware of the words on this screen right now. You are awareness right now. This witnessing presence that you are was never suffering, and will never be enlightened. This witnessing presence that you are right now watches the stories of Cameron and his suffering, and Cameron with his hopes of enlightenment. This witnessing presence cannot suffer, and it cannot attain enlightenment.

So, again, what do you do about the suffering stories of Cameron? You watch. And you know the stories are only imaginary. All psychological suffering is imaginary. The imaginary stories are free to come and go. You remain as the witnessing presence.

You may notice that all doubts are merely conceptual nonsense appearing in this present awareness. What to do? Nothing—just watch.

Cameron: To be honest, I am not sure this response goes to the heart of my question. It's clear that we are this witnessing presence, and the witnessing presence essentially doesn't suffer. However, if the ego story is still able to generate enough energy to get its hooks in, then there is suffering. And since we are down to basics here—the question is, is there psychological suffering or isn't there? It seems to me that witnessing is inevitable because we are the witness, even if it witnesses suffering.

My point is, if suffering is arising in the story it's because the 'I' illusion hasn't been seen through, otherwise, what would happen is— up would come conditions that normally amount to suffering, and a simple witnessing from peace would occur, because one is certain that the story is untrue.

If you believe in the story with the fixed, solidified self-entity then there is suffering. To say one should 'just watch' is all good and well, but what we are doing is watching suffering, and believe me I have been a Buddhist for many years and made it my business to watch that suffering really closely.

What I am interested in is seeing through the 'I' thought completely, so that when it arises strongly, I can stay firmly with the peace of my witnessing presence, firm in the knowledge of its fiction. If this 'I' patterning has the power to rise up and (seemingly) occlude the peace of awareness then this has not been done, has it?

Sorry, if I am getting difficult but this seems to be the axis on which all my doubts spin. If this is getting too involved for email discussion and you would prefer to chat on the phone (and have time do so) I would be happy to make a call at a convenient time in the future—maybe hearing it from a voice will fill the missing gap.

Stephen: Yes, I am happy to talk on the phone. Do you see that all psychological suffering is based in imagination? Do you see that even the story that I was suffering, I am suffering, or I may be suffering is also based in imagination? Do you see that your story (and mine) describing the process of psychological suffering is based in imagination? Describing the process of suffering was helpful to this point. Now see that it was all a story, all imagination.

There is no such thing as psychological suffering outside of thought or imagination. There is no such thing as enlightenment outside of thought or imagination. There is no separate entity called Cameron outside of thought or imagination. If you believe that psychological suffering was real in the past, then it can return and be real again in the future. But was it *ever* real? Or was it thought-based and imaginary? You may notice you really don't know what psychological suffering is, or if it has any reality.

If you see that suffering is all thought-based and imaginary, but still want to change the story—that is the dream character trying to control the dream. There is no separate Cameron creating or controlling the stories. See the dream story of suffering as a dream and just watch it.

There is no such thing as psychological suffering. There is no such thing as Cameron. So how can Cameron do anything about psychological suffering? These words are literal, and are not just a cute spiritual metaphor. All dreams are free to come and go through you including the dreams of suffering, and the dreams of freedom from suffering. They are all dreams.

Just watch. And *you have no idea* what you're watching! This *watching* that we are is absolutely clueless! It doesn't differentiate between suffering and peace. Knowing suffering from peace is mind-stuff. Suffering and freedom from suffering are both mind-stuff, and imaginary. This witnessing presence that we are is the only constant, the only reality.

Cameron: I have been letting this sink in, and I think I believed that in the 'occluded' state the suffering is real. What I am hearing you say is that suffering is not real, and you can't do anything to stop it from coming and going. You see, I think that's the thing. I was subtly

205

expecting something that would have no suffering in the sense that the story would be free of suffering.

That's it! I have no control over the story—even the suffering, it's not me. I can't stop it because it's not my business. I am simply the *seeing*. I have been thinking that my 'understanding' is in the story, and that it will change the story somehow. Wow, I can't stop the suffering, and I can't get free—it's all in the story. I think I am getting it. Let's talk on the telephone to make sure I'm getting this straight.

[After a phone conversation]

Cameron: Thanks for the chat. I see now what you were pointing out about this presence having nothing to do with thoughts about suffering or the blissful sensations. When you said the awareness that we are has no idea about suffering or peace, it clicked that it's just a complete openness that lets anything happen and it's always been here because things always just happen anyway.

Bondage and Liberation are creations of Maya, superimpositions upon the Brahman imagined by the mind without any existence in reality. The scriptures even proclaim aloud: "There is in truth no creation and no destruction; no one is bound, no one is seeking Liberation, no one is on the way to Deliverance. There are none Liberated. This is the absolute truth."
—**Shankara**

Everything is Self-Perfected in This

Cameron: I just want to let you know the pointing out was so clear last time there seems to be this entirely stable clarity now. The clincher was when you pointed out that even when the sense of 'I' and 'doing' arise there still is no one doing even that. It's complete freedom. It's so simple. It really just is *this*. Thoughts are being thought, sensations are happening in the body, but there is no one—just this luminous present.

Strangely, far from being detached, all the thoughts and emotions are so vivid. But it's like this raw energy. Even when my mind is very discursive and there are what seem to be negative stories, it's like the discursiveness is this torrent of energy and I really enjoy it. In my life situation I am going through a very stressful time of year, but there is just this vivid sense of being. And the more intense things get the more beautiful it seems.

As a Buddhist I used to often chant "Everything is self-perfected in the Dharmadatu (Sphere of Reality)" and never get it. I thought the Dharmadatu was this cool place you see when you are enlightened. Now I see what it means. It's astonishing.

Stephen: Yes, that's it exactly. Your description reminds me of Nisargadatta's description of this:

"It is solid, steady, changeless, beginning-less and endless, ever new, ever fresh.

"This reality is so concrete, so actual, so much more tangible than mind and matter, that compared to it, even a diamond is soft like butter. This overwhelming actuality makes the world dreamlike, misty, irrelevant.

"To me nothing ever happens. There is something changeless, motionless, immovable, rock-like, unassailable; a solid mass of pure being-consciousness-bliss. I am never out of it. Nothing can take me out of it, no torture, no calamity.

"My world is free from opposites, of mutually destructive discrepancies; harmony pervades; its peace is rocklike; this peace and silence are my body.

"My condition is absolutely steady. Whatever I may do, it stays like a rock—motionless. Once you have awakened into reality, you stay in it. It is self-evident and yet beyond description."

Cameron, he's describing *your* natural state, *my* natural state, *our* natural state. So many years struggling to discover this simplicity that was always here—I am this. It all makes sense now. So simple.

O grace abounding that had made me fit
to fix my eyes on the eternal light
until my vision was consumed in it!

I saw within its depth how it conceives
all things in a single volume bound by Love,
of which the universe is the scattered leaves;

Substance, accident, and their relation
so fused that all I say could do no more
than yield a glimpse of that bright revelation.

I think I saw the universal form
that binds these things, for as I speak these words
I feel my joy swell and my spirits warm.
—Dante

References for Quotations

Page	Source
13	The Old Testament, The Book of Exodus
17	Ashtavakra Gita, translated by John Richards
19	Song of Myself, Walt Whitman
21	I AM THAT, Nisargadatta Maharaj
23	The Zen Teachings of Huang Po, translated by John Blofeld
45	Poem "Who," Aurobindo, Sri Aurobindo Society
48	Essay on Robert Frost, Kahlil Gibran, NY Times, April 1982
51	Poem "Beyond the Silence," Aurobindo, Sri Aurobindo Society
52	The Essential Rumi, translation by Coleman Barks
54	The Upanishads, translated by Juan Mascaro
57	I AM THAT, Nisargadatta Maharaj
71	Ashtavakra Gita, translated by John Richards
78	The Unborn, Zen Master Bankei, translated by Norman Waddell
83	Poem "The Little Lamb," William Blake
84	The Over-Soul, Ralph Waldo Emerson
87	Ashtavakra Gita, translated by John Richards
89	The New Testament, The Book of Galatians
93	The Awakening of Intelligence, Jiddu Krishnamurti
96	The Dhammapada, translated by Juan Mascaro
98	The Crest Jewel of Wisdom, Shankara
100	Bhagavad Gita, translated by Juan Mascaro
102	I AM THAT, Nisargadatta Maharaj
103	The Old Testament, The Book of Genesis
108	Part One: Life, Emily Dickinson, The Complete Poems
110	The Zen Teachings of Huang Po, translated by John Blofeld
136	Part One: Life, Emily Dickinson, The Complete Poems
139	The Collected Works of Ramana Maharshi, edited by Arthur Osborne
143	The Old Testament, The Book of Isaiah
145	As You Like It, William Shakespeare
172	The Collected Works of Ramana Maharshi, edited by Arthur Osborne
176	Verses on Faith Mind, Seng-Tsan, translated by Richard B. Clarke
177	Albert Einstein
179	Tao Te Ching, The Essential Tao, translated by Thomas Cleary
181	The Awakening of Intelligence, Jiddu Krishnamurti
183	The Zen Teachings of Huang Po, translated by John Blofeld
186	I AM THAT, Nisargadatta Maharaj
187	Poem "On the Banks of a Rocky Stream," William Wordsworth
190	Verses on Faith Mind, Seng-Tsan, translated by Richard B. Clarke
194	Poem "Abode of the Beloved," Kabir
198	Bhagavad Gita, translated by Juan Mascaro
200	The Zen Teachings of Huang Po, translated by John Blofeld
206	The Crest Jewel of Wisdom, Shankara
208	The Divine Comedy, Dante

Books & Audio CDs from Atma Publishing

Books by Stephen Wingate:

The Outrageous Myths of Enlightenment
Writings, Dialogues & Correspondence on Non-duality
Paperback -205 pages ISBN 0-9787254-0-9
Author: Stephen Wingate

Dogs, Cats & Dreams of Spiritual Awakening
Dialogues from Live Talks on Non-duality
Paperback -212 pages ISBN-13: 978-0-9787254-1-9
Author: Stephen Wingate

Audio CDs of Talks with Stephen Wingate Recorded Live:

Most of the Dialogues recorded in the book *Dogs, Cats & Dreams of Spiritual Awakening* are transcribed from these Live Talks:

Stay with I Am – 1 hour 17 min Audio CD
Get Clear on This – 1 hour 8 min Audio CD
The Pit Bull is Dead – 1 hour 1 min Audio CD
I Am the Resolution to All Spiritual Seeking – 1 hr 16 min Audio CD
The Universe Says Meow – 1 hour Audio CD
Self-Realization, Liberation & Enlightenment – 1 hr 14min Audio CD
Neti-Neti – This Ain't It-That Ain't It – 1 hour 12 min Audio CD
The Fall from Grace – 1 hour 10 min Audio CD

Visit: www.**AtmaPublishing**.com
-Listen to samples from the Audio CDs
-Read excerpts from the Books

Visit Stephen Wingate's website:
www.**LivingInPeace-TheNaturalState**.com